Praise for *Inner Pathways to the Divine*

"Diane Toland calls these tarot cards teachers—and she is so right on. What a magical and novel way to approach this ancient path. I really like the affirmations she has created!"
—**LOUISE L. HAY**, author of *You Can Heal Your Life* and *Empowering Women*

"Diane's book is an inspiring new journey into an ancient experience of wisdom. She provides new and magical mirrors for the journey into higher consciousness. The tarot is a wonderful way to access our subconscious and intuitional experience."
—**LYNN V. ANDREWS**, author of *Love and Power* and *Medicine Woman*

"We are all mystical beings trying to understand the many aspects of our daily lives. The Tarot can be of great value in the search to know ourselves better. Without self knowledge, there can be no true growth. Ms. Toland approaches spiritual growth in a loving, warm and accessible way. The result is purely magical."
—**BETTY BETHARDS**, author of *The Dream Book, Be Your Own Guru*, and *There is No Death*.

"In *Inner Pathways to the Divine*, Diane Toland moves far beyond mere tolerance for a variety of spiritual paths. She abides in a place of devotion to the divine and delights in the myriad pathways toward the holy. Her creativity breathes new life into the journey, and simultaneously nurtures and challenges those who are walking and working on their spiritual path. I am thankful for the breadth of her devotion and wonder."
—Rev. **DR. SANDY WINTER**, minister *University Presbyterian Church* and *Student Center*

"Diane Toland's book is among those I would strongly recommend to people who wish to use the Tarot to assist them in their personal journey of self-exploration. She addresses the journey that the Tarot truly represents, that of the spirit toward self-realization, rather than using the cards as gamelike divination "magic." Anyone interested in Tarot, from beginner to seasoned practitioner, will benefit greatly from Diane's insights, questions and prompts. I thoroughly enjoyed reading *Inner Pathways to the Divine* having used Tarot cards for thirty years in my own spiritual practice and spiritual journey."

—**VIMALA MCCLURE**, author of *A Woman's Guide to Tantra Yoga*, *The Tao of Motherhood*, and *The Path of Parenting*.

"Like *The Artist's Way*, a tool for inner discovery. *Inner Pathways to the Divine* is a practical application of concrete plans and affirmations. A unique guide for revitalizing your inner life. Good for individual work and even better in a group. A unique and helpful structure for experienced pilgrims of the inner life, yet accessible for the curious beginner."

—Rev. **MARK J. GALLAGHER**, minister *Unitarian Universalist Church*

"Those of us who are seeking enlightenment find a person skilled and knowledgeable in their chosen field, and we wish them to *do it for us*. But, in this book, Diane has empowered us with her simple directions to *do it for ourselves*. A great leader isn't one who has many followers, but one who teaches others to be great leaders as well. Through a desire to serve humanity, she has taken the often misunderstood subject of tarot and made it sage and easy to understand. Loving warmth and the beauty of her soul shine on every page."

—**GLORIA D. BENISH**, Ph.D., author of *Go Within or Go Without* and *To Become as Little Children*.

"An enlightening and enjoyable book. It is an inspirational approach to shaping our destiny. Diane Toland emphasizes the spiritual perspective of the Major Arcana as a positive key to finding our path on life's journey. It shows readers how to use their own creativity to produce a happier and more fulfilling life."

—**CRYSTINA O'BRIEN**, Australian author of *Chronic Fatigue Busters* and *Dress for Success*.

Inner Pathways to the Divine

Exploring your Spiritual Self
through the Tarot's Major Mentors

By Diane Toland

SunShine Press Publications

SunShine Press Publications, Inc.
P. O. Box 333
Hygiene, CO 80533
Web: www.sunshinepress.com
Email: sunshinepress@sunshinepress.com

Artwork, "Inward Journey" by Barbara D. Boss
Coeur d'Alene, Idaho 83815
Cover design by Michel Kiteley
Longmont, Colorado 80501

Publisher's Cataloging-in-Publication Data

Toland, Diane.
   Inner pathways to the divine : exploring your spiritual self
   through the tarot's major mentors / Diane Toland
p. cm.
   1. Spirituality 2. Tarot I. Title
   Includes bibliographical references
   ISBN: 1-888604-17-4
BF1879.T2J39   133.3'2424   2001086776

Printed in the United States
5 4 3 2 1
Printed on recycled acid-free papers using soy ink

Dedication

To my husband, Terry, for believing in me.
I love you with all my heart and soul.

Table of Contents

Chapter 1

Introduction to Pathworking with the Tarot

Mirror, Mirror on the Wall

Imagine moving down a corridor lined with 22 magic mirrors. Picture yourself gazing into each of those mirrors to find a specific aspect of yourself reflected back to you. A name appears at the bottom of each mirror's ornate frame and you begin to understand how the characters before you fit into the complexity of your own personality. Even more than that, you see the reflected images as archetypes, significant representatives from the collective unconscious we all share.

Major Mentors

Within the 78 cards of the traditional tarot deck, there are 22 major arcana or trump cards. These cards are the most important images in the deck because they represent the soul's journey through consciousness. Consider them as 22 teachers or mentors—*major mentors*—in your life's work. You've heard the expression, "When the student is ready, the teacher will come." Well, the teachers are here. They exist in a rich tapestry of medieval symbolism, eagerly waiting to assist you on your spiritual journey.

Beyond Divination

The tarot has long been associated primarily with divination, or fortune-telling. But the tarot is so much more than a means to gain insight into the future. Relegating the tarot cards to the role of fortune-telling is like using a samurai sword to make a sandwich. The sword could serve that use, but it was certainly designed for a much different purpose. The major mentors provide symbolism that touches our souls and speaks to us on many levels. I believe that we change our futures every moment of every day when we make decisions and take action. We also create our futures when we adopt certain beliefs or choose *not* to take any action. We are like sculptors molding clay or chipping marble. We dynamically create our realities while we live our lives. The tarot can be an effective tool for shedding light on an existing situation or frame of mind. It can help us to gain insight into what might be a possible future if we continued to do what we are currently doing or believe what we are currently believing. It can be a vehicle for clairvoyance or other such perception. But, it is much, much more than simply a divinatory tool.

What I propose in this book is that the tarot can be used in a deeper, more profound way. The tarot can be used to bring us closer to our Divinity by offering us a mirror into ourselves. Gaining insight into ourselves helps us to gain clarity into our life's purpose and our relationship with our Creator. This type of focus brings us closer to gratitude, to love, and to a state of Divine Grace. If you are seeking to understand your own personal spiritual experience, your own path to the Divine, then you have come to the right place. The tarot is a tremendous tool to help you find your own spiritual path.

Sacred Symbols in our Past, Present, and Future

Why use the characters from tarot cards? It certainly would have been simpler to use a less controversial series of pictures. Why not use Greek Olympians or Roman Gods/Goddesses? Why not choose modern fairy tale characters or Pre-Christian Goddesses or some other mythological characters? Certainly, archetypal images are plentiful; they're all around us. In fact, they exist in some form in every known mythology. However, I chose the controversial and often misunderstood tarot because Judeo-Christian thought and belief is one of our most influential social and theological experiences here in the west. The tarot cards depict a great deal of symbolism from Judeo-Christian theology. In fact, many of the tarot's illustrations are Biblical in origin. This is not to say that the symbology is limited to Judeo-Christian thought. Rather, it is a rich amalgam of *many* esoteric systems, both eastern and western in origin. The tarot's symbols speak to us in a way that touches us very deeply.

The Rider-Waite Tarot Deck®

The tarot is a profound tool that is available to all of us. The cards I have chosen to use as a companion to this book are from the Rider-Waite Tarot Deck[1] (also known as the Rider Tarot Deck), created in 1910 by Arthur E. Waite and illustrated by Pamela Colman Smith. The Rider-Waite Tarot Deck is filled with vivid symbolism and beautiful imagery. And, although the illustrations depict medieval life with peasants, court and clergy, the clear roles of the characters provide guidance and relevance in today's modern world. So that you may fully experience the vivid imagery of the cards, I urge you to purchase your own Rider-Waite Tarot Deck as soon as you can so you may use it to explore the archetypes. This book will provide black and white illustrations for you, but it will not be nearly as beneficial or convenient as having the cards in front of you in full color.

After completing the process outlined in the book, I encourage you to delve into the enormous pool of other artists' renderings available in addition to the Rider-Waite deck. Indeed, there are a myriad of decks available. As a woman, I personally love tarot decks like the round Motherpeace[2] cards because they are filled with images that especially resonate for women. I also have a great appreciation for diverse imagery from other cultures and have gained a great deal of insight from many of the unique decks available today. As you explore the various decks, you will find that each is deeply meaningful and brimming with artistic illustrations. So, find a tarot deck that speaks to you personally and get to know its characters. Keep in mind, though, that a true tarot deck includes 78 cards—22 are major arcana cards, and 56 are minor arcana cards (which are divided into four suits, usually depicted as cups, pentacles, swords, and wands). There are many other card decks and "oracles" that don't fit into this authentic format. You may find them to be excellent cards for providing insight, but they are not actual tarot cards.

Origins of the Tarot

Some mystics insist, citing legend, that the tarot originated in Ancient Egypt, as engraved plates of ancient knowledge or as a sacred book that escaped the burning of the Alexandrian library. There is some mystery surrounding its earliest origins. But what we do know for a fact is that, by the fourteenth century, tarot images had reached Spain, Italy, and France, and were transported to other countries by the Romany or "gypsy" people who used them primarily for the purposes of fortune telling. The closest we can get to an actual date of origin is 1392, the time of their first recorded usage. In this year, Charles VI of France commissioned an artist named Jaquemin Gringonneur to provide him with three sets of the major arcana of 22 cards.[3] Due to the period's most powerful patriarchal influence, the Roman Catholic Church, the illustrations portrayed the European feudal system of the time with clergy, royalty, merchants, craftsmen, and peasants. The cards are said to contain sacred knowledge from Ancient Egypt, India, Greece, and, largely, from the early Judeo-Christian mysteries.

A Picture Speaks a Thousand Words

Pictures can say so much more than words could ever begin to reveal because they have such unique effects on different individuals. I could describe, define, or name a color to you, for example, and you would have *some* understanding of it. However, if you saw the color before you, your experience would be much more profound. Seeing the color would provide you with a much fuller understanding of it. Upon viewing the color red, for example, you might have strong feelings and vivid memories. You might remember a red wagon from your childhood and the joy associated with youthful play. You might have non-specific feelings about passion and intensity that you associate with that vivid color. The color itself might even be a springboard, catapulting you into a myriad of related thoughts and feelings. Carl Jung worked with symbolism as a means to unlock the door to the subconscious mind, to understand ourselves, the world around us, and the personal spiritual experience. It was he who brought us the understanding of archetypes and their social and psychological significance.

The symbolism of the tarot's major arcana is archetypal in nature. Archetypes are those symbols that are so significant, they exist in the collective unconscious that we all share. According to Marion Weinstein, "the tarot works by means of *mnemonics*—a system which triggers the memory and the resources of one's subconscious mind by the use of visual imagery.... The symbols of the tarot came from the world of dreams, the collective unconscious, the depths of the Universe itself—from all of life. They speak to us...in intimate and personal ways."[4]

Pathworking

Pathworking is a term that refers to the actions we take or the work we do while traversing our paths. We use the word "path" as an analogy for the spiritual journey, our soul's movement through consciousness, as well as our body's movement through the physical world. We all have our own, very personal, spiritual goals. We seek to better know God or to become one with the Universe. We seek to walk the path laid out by Buddha or Jesus or Mohammed or one of our history's greatest avatars. We seek to be better people, to infuse our hearts with love and to clear our personalities of negative characteristics like selfishness and jealousy. Whatever our goals, we walk our paths every day. Some days, we might take giant leaps toward the Divine. Other days, perhaps we take a few steps backward. But, by consciously working our path or "pathworking," we commit to take some action each and every day. When we accomplish this, we elevate our spiritual journey to a position of high priority in our lives. And we move ever closer to realizing our dream of achieving union with the Divine.

The Sacred Journey is the Goal

The purpose of the journey described in this book is to provide you with many magic mirrors into yourself. As you journey through the experiences of the 22 mentors, you will become closer to yourself and your own Divinity. Some people have a very specific relationship to God, while others take a broader approach to their spirituality. I personally believe that there are infinite roads to the Divine. However, you have your own personal beliefs and religious affiliations (or not). So I encourage you to discover and earnestly walk your own way to the Divine. The tarot is simply a tool—an excellent one that can be used to better understand ourselves, our world, and our relationship to God or the Divine.

Exploring yourself and your spiritual purpose through the "mirrors" of the tarot's archetypes does not constitute a religion of any sort. If you are concerned about the "occult" associations with tarot, you may be more comfortable approaching your study of the tarot's 22 mentors as a psychological pursuit. Psychology and spirituality do not really oppose each other, especially when one guides you more deeply into the other. Consider science and spirituality as seen by Albert Einstein, probably the most gifted scientific mind of our time. Einstein found himself increasingly humbled and awed—closer to God—the more he learned about science and the laws of the universe. So, perhaps by studying ourselves, we will come to find the Divine within us, that luminous spark which links us to the Source of that Divinity.

It is my belief that there is no greater work in our human existence than to become connected to our own Divinity for, truly, God/dess resides within all of us. It doesn't matter what we call the Divine or Divinity—God is God whether we use the term Goddess or Great Spirit or Supreme Being or Universe. So, in this book I will primarily use the terms "Divinity" and "Divine" in order to be as inclusive as possible. As you read, mentally replace the word I've used with the one that speaks to your own heart. It's your journey and for each of us, our own journey is the critical one. Each of our spiritual experiences is varied, unique, and incredibly personal, as will be your personal journey through the lessons of the mentors. Travelling the path to illumination is an exciting and profound journey, and you may already be aware of this because your steps have already begun.

Chapter 2

Self-Exploration and the Major Mentors

Getting Acquainted With Yourself

In order for you to fully understand the relevance of the tarot's major mentors in your life and spiritual journey, you'll need to get to know their characteristics, their subtleties, and the unique messages they have to impart. You'll need to fully experience the archetypes by exploring the aspects of yourself that they represent. This is why I have integrated both inner work and outer work into this chapter to enhance your learning process. I have also provided you with several different modalities of expression to effectively reinforce your understanding of the mentors.

The Process

For each of the 22 mentors, the self-exploration process will be comprised of certain specific steps. The process begins with a brief description of the tarot illustration and its unique symbolism. Then, by contemplating deeply and answering honestly five questions about yourself, your spiritual path, and your life experience, you will fully experience the messages of each mentor, as well as the part of you that relates to the character or illustration. After answering the questions, you will read an affirmation that defines the beliefs associated with each mentor, and will add your own personal affirmation to reinforce the positive message. This process of defining your beliefs is a critical step in clarifying your path to the Divine. The reason for this is that your values and beliefs define not only who you are, but dictate the nature of your path. When you have completed answering the questions and writing your affirmation, you will choose a piece of art, music, or literature that speaks to the message of each mentor. Then, to conclude your process, you will choose an image from a magazine, a photograph, or an item that represents the mentor to you. When you have fully explored all 22 cards, you will design your own, personal tarot mandala, made of the images you chose yourself, to create an artistic visual representation of your spiritual self and your spiritual journey. You will also have the opportunity to outwardly express the message of each mentor by taking some specific action in your life and in your world.

Before You Begin

The renowned philosopher and mystic George Gurdjieff taught that our primary responsibility in life is to work on ourselves spiritually. He believed that we spend most of our lives running on a sort of automatic pilot, and are asleep to our true selves. I certainly agree with Gurdjieff that there could be no work more vital than the process of heightening our awareness and understanding our relationship to our Divine Source. The format of this chapter is somewhat like a workbook, but I urge you not to see the activities ahead as *work*, per se. The kind of work that is ahead of you is really more like play. The process itself is fun and exciting, and what you have to gain from your diligence is a huge amount of growth and awareness. So, I hope that you will approach your learning process with eagerness, high spirits, and childlike delight.

Full Lives

Your life is already full, I know. You're incredibly busy, just like me. Remember that any progress you make represents real growth. Doing something is better than doing nothing. Any steps you take toward completing the process, even if they are small, are steps in the right direction. So, don't get overwhelmed or overly concerned that you might not have time to complete the whole process. Just dive in and enjoy it. Do as much as you can. I honestly believe that you will have so much fun and will find the process so deepening that you will suddenly find time in your busy schedule to finish one mentor, then another, and another still. Before you know it, you'll have completed them all and will be moving on to the chapter on practical applications for your new-found knowledge. I know you'll be so enthusiastic about creating your own tarot mandala that you'll design your meaningful piece of art as soon as you have collected the 22 images. So, just begin. You have much to gain and nothing to lose.

Getting the Most out of This Chapter

If you were to review a tarot dictionary that describes the varied images of some different tarot decks or read several dream interpretation books, you might be surprised to find that there is little consistency among "authorities" on the subject of interpreting symbols. You might be exasperated to find symbols being given different or even contradictory interpretations. I have provided you with interpretations from a variety of sources, some of which resonate for me personally. However, I encourage you to use your own knowledge, personal experience, and intuition to interpret the cards. The power and profundity of symbols is vast, because words can't possibly speak for them adequately. Therefore, trust in the richness of those symbols and let your own heart, mind, and intuition be your guide.

As you answer the questions, you may find that you have difficulty answering one or several. If you find yourself getting stuck, just move on. Thinking about the question is like planting a seed. You may find the answer sprouting up in your mind when you least expect it. You can always come back and answer the question later. I always find that it's better to maintain momentum and keep working, rather than to focus too greatly on one question. Also, if a question calls for a numbered list (for example, "list twenty things you consider beautiful or attractive"), and you can only name a few, list as many as you can and move on. Later, you may find that other ideas come to mind. Posing the question to yourself is, in itself, an important part of the exercise. You may find that your responses reveal themselves over a period of time.

It is best to experience the mentors in their given order, but it is not essential. If you are drawn to a particular illustration or wish to choose your own order, go right ahead. Write your answers and observations on paper or type them into a computer. Do record them, though. You will want to have a record of your growth and progress for future reference. If you wish, read the entire book, then come back and complete the process. Experience the mentors in whatever way suits you. This is your process. Most of all, remember that this is an adventure into your inner world. It is a tremendous opportunity to create a clearer path toward the Divine. So, enjoy your journey.

The Mentors

0. The Fool
1. The Magician
2. The High Priestess
3. The Empress
4. The Emperor
5. The Heirophant
6. The Lovers
7. The Chariot
8. Strength
9. The Hermit
10. Wheel of Fortune
11. Justice
12. The Hanged Man
13. Death
14. Temperance
15. The Devil
16. The Tower
17. The Star
18. The Moon
19. The Sun
20. Judgement
21. The World

THE FOOL.

0. The Fool

Description

A Fool, dressed as one who is taking a journey, carries a small travelling bundle on his shoulder. Walking happily toward the edge of a cliff, he is unaware or perhaps unconcerned that the ground under his feet is about to disappear. A dog, representing the instincts, leaps at his heels in an effort to warn him of the impending danger. The Fool wears on his face an expression of serenity and trust. He appears not to have a care in the world, and believes that all will be well. He is fully prepared to take his "leap of faith" and trusts completely in the universe. Some say the Fool is the pivot or central figure around whom all of the other major mentors revolve.

Self-Exploration

1. Look at the card and note how it makes you feel. Do you like this character?
2. Can you relate to the feelings of serenity and peace the Fool exudes?
3. Do you remember a time or experience when you have felt the surety of the fool's easy steps? Have you ever risen above your basic instincts and simply trusted the Universe/the Divine to supply you with the support you needed to take that next step? Describe the experience of embracing this child-like trust and reflect upon how it made you feel.
4. Is there a "leap of faith" you wish you could take in your life, but are held back by fear or rationality? If you were to jump off the cliff and trust that all would be well, what might happen? Explore both your hopes and your fears when answering this question.
5. It is said that the fool carries with him a traveling bag containing the four suits of the minor arcana, which represent the four elements of earth, air, fire, and water. These four elements represent the physical

world, the mind, power/intuition, and emotions, respectively. If you were the fool in the picture, what would you be carrying in the bundle attached to the staff? How would it help you on your spiritual journey?

Affirmation

Our beliefs create our reality. Write a personal affirmation that reflects your beliefs seen through the mirror of this major mentor. I have provided one for you.

I trust in the Universe.

Action

You have explored your thoughts and feelings by answering the questions above. This has been your inner work. Now, as part of your outer work, take some action! Perform an activity, action, or ritual that relates to the lessons of this card. It will help you to fully experience the message of the card as well as the aspect of yourself represented by the archetype. I have provided some examples. After completing the task, note your observations.

- Do something outrageous, foolish, or out of character.
- Trust. Do something that requires a leap of faith.
- Spend some time with a newborn baby or young child. Reflect on the child's innocence, authenticity, and perfection.

Art

Art touches the soul. Select a song, a poem, or a piece of art, literature, or film that relates to this card. Describe its relevance.

Mandala

In Chapter 4, you will create a personal tarot mandala. Select an image that exemplifies this card. Take a photograph or draw a picture. Choose an existing photo, a magazine picture, or an item that personally illustrates the card to you.

THE MAGICIAN.

I. The Magician

Description

The magician stands in a fine robe before a table of magical implements. These are the tools of his craft and represent the four elements of earth, air, fire, and water. Earth corresponds to the physical realm, while air represents the intellect. Fire corresponds to action and intuition, while water represents the emotional realm. The Magician is an able practitioner of the craft of creating as well as seeing through illusion. He holds a wand above his head and points to the earth below. Around him are roses, signifying passion, and lilies, signifying purity. Atop his head is the infinity sign.

Self-Exploration

1. Look at the card and note how it makes you feel. Do you like this character?
2. The magical premise, "As above, so below; As within, so without" applies to the gesture the Magician makes. He believes that he alone manifests his reality. And as his actions influence his life, it is his thoughts and beliefs that actually create his world. List ten ways in which your thoughts or beliefs have helped to create your current reality. An example might be that you believed that you were capable of something and, hence, have been successful. Another might be that you have been limited in your life because of a limiting belief. Be as specific as possible.
3. Is there something in your life you would like to take control of? If you were the Magician, how would you accomplish this?
4. What new skills would you like to master? In what way would these new skills or this new mastery help you to create a better life for yourself?

5. Fully experiencing the spiritual journey requires the elements of purity and passion. In what ways would you consider yourself a purist? What are you most passionate about? Take some time to consider this and note as many examples as you can.

Affirmation

Our beliefs create our reality. Write a personal affirmation that reflects your beliefs seen through the mirror of this major mentor. I have provided one for you.

My thoughts create my world by manifesting my reality.

Action

You have explored your thoughts and feelings by answering the questions above. This has been your inner work. Now, as part of your outer work, take some action! Perform an activity, action, or ritual that relates to the lessons of this card. It will help you to fully experience the message of the card as well as the aspect of yourself represented by the archetype. I have provided some examples. After completing the task, note your observations.

- Post affirmations in key locations around your house in an effort to focus on the positive beliefs that help you to create a positive world.
- Collect something to represent each of the four elements to you and place them on a table or shelf before you like the Magician in the illustration.
- Assert your independence in some way. This is a powerful and profound action.

Art

Art touches the soul. Select a song, a poem, or a piece of art, literature, or film that relates to this card. Describe its relevance.

Mandala

In Chapter 4, you will create a personal tarot mandala. Select an image that exemplifies this card. Take a photograph or draw a picture. Choose an existing photo, a magazine picture, or an item that personally illustrates the card to you.

THE HIGH PRIESTESS.

II. The High Priestess

Description

The High Priestess sits on a throne between two pillars of light and dark, representing mercy and severity, the poles of extremes. She wears on her head the crown of the full moon, while her foot rests upon the lunar crescent. This is the temple or vestal virgin who pulls from her cloak the book of the sacred law and wears upon her breast the equal-armed cross of central balance. Behind her is a veil of pomegranates and palms, indicating the polarity of masculine and feminine energies,[5] of yin and yang. Some tarot decks call this "The Papess," referring to either Visconti Papess or Pope Joan. A great deal of controversy exists regarding their existence within the leadership of the 9th and 14th century Roman Catholic Church.[6]

Self-Exploration

1. Look at the card and note how it makes you feel. Do you like this character?

2. The High Priestess is a spiritual teacher/guide who opens doors and provides advice to the seeker. She is a wise, intelligent woman who provides inspiration and revelation. Has there been a wise woman in your past that has offered you counsel? What wisdom has she imparted to you and have you taken her message seriously? Is there a wise woman in your life now? If you cannot identify such a woman in your life, perhaps there is someone that you admire (living person or fictional character) for her wisdom and intelligence. If that woman were to counsel you now, what advice do you think she would offer?

3. The High Priestess is said to symbolize the veiled aspect of woman, her secrecy and mystery. What secrets within you need to be revealed?

4. What potential is not yet fulfilled in you?
5. The human psyche contains both masculine (yang) and feminine (yin) components. Men and women have within them both aspects. The High Priestess relates to inner femininity, while the Empress (next card) relates to outer femininity. What might you do to better nurture the feminine nature that exists deep within you?

Affirmation

Our beliefs create our reality. Write a personal affirmation that reflects your beliefs seen through the mirror of this major mentor. I have provided one for you.

Inner wisdom is my birthright.

Action

You have explored your thoughts and feelings by answering the questions above. This has been your inner work. Now, as part of your outer work, take some action! Perform an activity, action, or ritual that relates to the lessons of this card. It will help you to fully experience the message of the card as well as the aspect of yourself represented by the archetype. I have provided some examples. After completing the task, note your observations.

- Stand before a mirror and affirm your inner beauty. Name at least 10 beautiful things.
- Share a secret about yourself that needs to be revealed. Perhaps some light needs to be shed in a dark place. Be responsible, courageous and compassionate.
- Create a meaningful ceremony to celebrate a teenager's advancement into adulthood. The process of initiation is sacred to the High Priestess character.

Art

Art touches the soul. Select a song, a poem, or a piece of art, literature, or film that relates to this card. Describe its relevance.

Mandala

In Chapter 4, you will create a personal tarot mandala. Select an image that exemplifies this card. Take a photograph or draw a picture. Choose an existing photo, a magazine picture, or an item that personally illustrates the card to you.

III. The Empress

Description

A beautiful, pregnant woman crowned with stars sits upon an opulent throne surrounded by nature's splendor. This is the archetypal Mother Goddess who brings forth life and ideas and symbolizes the pathway of birth and generation. The Empress wields an orb placed atop a scepter, indicating the exaltation of feminine energy within her jurisdiction. The waterfall in the distance represents the power of the emotions while the symbol of Venus reminds us of the power of beauty and attraction, of passion and love.

Self-Exploration

1. Look at this card and note how it makes you feel. Do you like this character?

2. There are many feminine characteristics that lend civility to a society. The Empress creates happiness, pleasure, beauty, and abundance by expressing her femininity in an outward manner. What feminine characteristics affect society in general and your life in particular? In what ways is our civilization more "civilized" because of the influence of women? Some examples of characteristics might be graciousness, elegance, gentleness, luxury and loving kindness.

3. The Empress symbolizes new life and the power of creation. What new idea yearns to be born within you and brought forth into the light?

4. In what ways do you connect with nature? Is it an emotional connection? What are you attracted to? Name twenty things that you consider beautiful and/or attractive.

5. Love is the fundamental law of the universe. In her maternal aspect, the Empress overflows with love and kindness toward others. How do you personally shower others with kindness and love? If you reserve these feelings for only a few close people in your life, what could you do to help you feel more loving toward others?

Affirmation

Our beliefs create our reality. Write a personal affirmation that reflects your beliefs seen through the mirror of this major mentor. I have provided one for you.

My cup overflows with love, beauty and abundance.

Action

You have explored your thoughts and feelings by answering the questions above. This has been your inner work. Now, as part of your outer work, take some action! Perform an activity, action, or ritual that relates to the lessons of this card. It will help you to fully experience the message of the card as well as the aspect of yourself represented by the archetype. I have provided some examples. After completing the task, note your observations.

- Stand before a mirror and affirm your outer beauty. Name at least 10 beautiful things.
- Play in the dirt. Plant some beautiful flowers or nourishing vegetables.
- Read some love poetry, a romantic novel, or watch a romantic movie.
- Express love to someone. Nurture and care for someone.
- Affirm nature's abundance in some way. Buy a big bushel of fruit, give gifts, be prosperous, celebrate! Prepare a nourishing meal for someone, highlighting nature's bounty.

Art

Art touches the soul. Select a song, a poem, or a piece of art, literature, or film that relates to this card. Describe its relevance.

Mandala

In Chapter 4, you will create a personal tarot mandala. Select an image that exemplifies this card. Take a photograph or draw a picture. Choose an existing photo, a magazine picture, or an item that personally illustrates the card to you.

IV. The Emperor

Description

The wise Emperor sits upon a throne adorned with the fiery rams of Aries. He holds a scepter and an orb representing his ability to wield his power in a balanced manner. His kingdom is vast, described by the distant mountains. He is a fair and compassionate ruler. And, although he is an advocate of peace, he remains ever willing to do battle to protect his people. Hence, he is shown wearing armor. His red robe symbolizes passion for his regal purpose.

Self-Exploration

1. Look at this card and note how it makes you feel. Do you like this character?

2. The Emperor is the quintessential leader archetype, advocating wisdom, consistency, fairness, and the necessity of putting the needs of one's subjects before one's own desires. This character is strong, yet understanding. We are all leaders in our own ways and have direct or indirect effects on others. How could you be a better leader? In what ways have you been disappointed by the leaders in your life (bosses, teachers, politicians, parents)?

3. The expression, "It's lonely at the top" relates well to the Emperor and the scepter he wields. Remember a time when your convictions have isolated you from others.

4. The fiery robe of leadership is not always comfortable to wear, but when we muster the courage to accept its weight, we elevate ourselves to the level of warrior/ess. Describe an experience when you have pulled this kind of courage from within and expressed yourself in this manner.

5. The Emperor is peaceful, yet wears armor, indicating that he is ever ready to do battle for what is right or to defend the righteous. When have you, like the ram on the Emperor's throne, bucked horns with an opponent? Where do you draw the line and believe that battle is necessary?

Affirmation

Our beliefs create our reality. Write a personal affirmation that reflects your beliefs seen through the mirror of this major mentor. I have provided one for you.

I am a responsible leader; I place the needs of others before my own desires.

Action

You have explored your thoughts and feelings by answering the questions above. This has been your inner work. Now, as part of your outer work, take some action! Perform an activity, action, or ritual that relates to the lessons of this card. It will help you to fully experience the message of the card as well as the aspect of yourself represented by the archetype. I have provided some examples. After completing the task, note your observations.

- Take the lead in a situation in which you are usually a follower. This is a powerful act.
- Support a leader in your community.
- Stand up and defend the righteous. Be a ram and buck horns if necessary.

Art

Art touches the soul. Select a song, a poem, or a piece of art, literature, or film that relates to this card. Describe its relevance.

Mandala

In Chapter 4, you will create a personal tarot mandala. Select an image that exemplifies this card. Take a photograph or draw a picture. Choose an existing photo, a magazine picture, or an item that personally illustrates the card to you.

THE HIEROPHANT.

© 1971 U.S. Games

V. The Heirophant

Description

Dressed in his traditional papal vestments, the church's leader sits on a throne, offering benediction to the monks seated before him. The Heirophant represents organized religion and the search for spiritual purpose. The keys below his feet indicate that the path can be a true one, and can enable us to achieve union with the Divine. The staff held by the Heirophant and the pillars on both sides of his throne represent the four elements and the position of central balance between opposite forces. The monks are said to represent obedience as well as our own intellectual and desire natures.[7]

Self-Exploration

1. Look at the card and note how it makes you feel. Do you like these characters?
2. Do you have something to learn from organized religion and can it help to guide you on your spiritual path? Has it taught you something in your past and do you believe it can teach you something in the future?
3. Where in your life do you need more structure, order, and obedience?
4. List at least five ways you can incorporate ritual into your daily life. Examples might be ritual cleansing while bathing, celebrating the change of seasons, or praying over your food to give thanks.
5. As you seek to understand your own personal spiritual philosophy and truth, you will encounter teachers along the way. Reflect upon some teachers who have guided you in the past. In what ways have they helped you? If you could manifest a teacher into your life today, what characteristics would this person have and what would he or she teach you?

Affirmation

Our beliefs create our reality. Write a personal affirmation that reflects your beliefs seen through the mirror of this major mentor. I have provided one for you.

My mind hears and understands the language of sacred truth.

Action

You have explored your thoughts and feelings by answering the questions above. This has been your inner work. Now, as part of your outer work, take some action! Perform an activity, action, or ritual that relates to the lessons of this card. It will help you to fully experience the message of the card as well as the aspect of yourself represented by the archetype. I have provided some examples. After completing the task, note your observations.

- Visit a church or place of worship that you have never visited before.
- Explore a new, perhaps mystical or esoteric, aspect of your own religion.
- Write a letter to thank a teacher who was important to you— someone who helped you to become the person you are today.
- Become a teacher to someone. Make a difference in someone's life.
- Practice obedience by obeying someone worthy of your trust, without question.

Art

Art touches the soul. Select a song, a poem, or a piece of art, literature, or film that relates to this card. Describe its relevance.

Mandala

In Chapter 4, you will create a personal tarot mandala. Select an image that exemplifies this card. Take a photograph or draw a picture. Choose an existing photo, a magazine picture, or an item that personally illustrates the card to you.

VI. The Lovers

Description

An angel hovers above a woman and a man. Behind them stands the earthly tree of knowledge and the fiery tree of inspiration. The symbols in this illustration relate to the forces of feminine and masculine (yin and yang) which can be reconciled to create a balanced wholeness within us. They further represent the natures of woman and man which, when joined, can create a love that is pure and whole. The mountain in the distance indicates the summits the pair are to climb together.[8] For the individual, the distant peaks represent the challenges one faces in the quest for inner harmony and integration of the two poles of extremes. It is often said that there is a choice described in the image of the Lovers and that the angel awaits the seeker's decision.

Self-Exploration

1. Look at the card and note how it makes you feel. Do you like these characters?

2. Do you feel that the masculine and feminine forces, the yin and the yang, the passive and the dynamic, are balanced within you? If not, which overshadows the other and how might you begin to bring them into harmony?

3. The Lovers card is often depicted as a man with two women, indicating a love affair with a trial or choice attached. Can you relate to the often conditional nature of love affairs and the many choices we have to make to embrace a love that is real and true? Note your thoughts. Then, describe a life experience that relates to this.

4. Loving each other as well as ourselves can bring us closer to the

41

Divine than any other action. Indeed, the nature of love is magical, spiritual, and altogether infinite. Contemplate the nature of love and the way in which it connects us to God/Spirit/the Divine and note your observations.

5. The Angel above the Lovers represents the spiritual nature of love. Discuss an experience when you felt Divinely guided, assisted, or inspired in a matter of love. (Remember that romantic love is not the only worthy expression of love. Consider love's full spectrum when answering this question.)

Affirmation

Our beliefs create our reality. Write a personal affirmation that reflects your beliefs seen through the mirror of this major mentor. I have provided one for you.

I am balanced and whole and ever worthy of love.

Action

You have explored your thoughts and feelings by answering the questions above. This has been your inner work. Now, as part of your outer work, take some action! Perform an activity, action, or ritual that relates to the lessons of this card. It will help you to fully experience the message of the card as well as the aspect of yourself represented by the archetype. I have provided some examples. After completing the task, note your observations.

- Let your heart make an important choice or decision for you.
- Make a list of 10 reasons why you are an incredibly loving person. Read the list to a trusted friend, lover, or family member.
- Tell someone that you love him or her, especially someone you have never told before. Express your love without expectation of a similar expression in return. Again, this does not need to be an expression of romantic love. It could be the love of a friend or family member, for example.

Art

Art touches the soul. Select a song, a poem, or a piece of art, literature, or film that relates to this card. Describe its relevance.

Mandala

In Chapter 4, you will create a personal tarot mandala. Select an image that exemplifies this card. Take a photograph or draw a picture. Choose an existing photo, a magazine picture, or an item that personally illustrates the card to you.

THE CHARIOT.

VII. The Chariot

Description

A brave warrior rides in a war chariot drawn by two opposite sphinxes, representing duality. Upon the warrior's head is a crown of stars, while crescent moons adorn his shoulders. He stands under a canopy of stars and holds the wand of will, which tames the beasts before him. Behind him is a vast city. However, he has crossed over a body of water and has, thus, chosen to leave the world of form to traverse the uncharted territory of consciousness.[9] He understands that the foes who are most worthy of facing are those which exist within.

Self-Exploration

1. Look at the card and note how it makes you feel. Do you like this character?
2. The Chariot card depicts the potential for victory against inner and outer conflicts. Which outer conflicts are you ready to face with the courage and skill of the Charioteer? Which inner conflicts are you ready to face?
3. The spiritual path can be seen as a warrior's path, because it requires strength, courage, perseverance, and momentum. How could the analogy of the warrior/ess assist you in your spiritual path today? How would you personally define victory?
4. The Chariot mentor is ruled by the astrological sign of Cancer. Therefore, intuition and emotion permeate all aspects of its message. The canopy of the chariot is decorated with stars, indicating such influences and psychic awareness. When have you used intuition or other "celestial" signposts to guide you on your journey? Might you

pay better attention to them? List four ways you could incorporate such influences into your daily life. Examples might be to pay attention to signs/omens and meaningful coincidences in your daily life or to trust your intuition and dreams.

5. The Charioteer leaves behind the mundane world, as illustrated by his journey across the waters of consciousness. If you were to embark on a similar journey into an altered state of consciousness, such as a vision quest, what format would you use? Would you go out into nature? Would you choose a special place of retreat? Contemplate a personal vision quest from a variety of angles. Where would you sleep? Would you use prayer, music, dance, or art? What special challenges would you face? Describe in detail a personal quest or retreat of this type.

Affirmation

Our beliefs create our reality. Write a personal affirmation that reflects your beliefs seen through the mirror of this major mentor. I have provided one for you.

I move triumphantly toward illumination.

Action

You have explored your thoughts and feelings by answering the questions above. This has been your inner work. Now, as part of your outer work, take some action! Perform an activity, action, or ritual that relates to the lessons of this card. It will help you to fully experience the message of the card as well as the aspect of yourself represented by the archetype. I have provided some examples. After completing the task, note your observations.

- Take a stand. Fight for a noble cause that you truly believe in. Join a battle that is worth fighting passionately. March, attend a rally, stuff envelopes. Get involved.

- Spend an entire day paying extra attention to the "celestial" influences that come into your view. Write down your dreams and daydreams. Follow your intuition. Trust your feelings.

- Embark on a vision quest. Surmount a personal challenge and endeavor to seek a deep, emotional, spiritual experience.

Art

Art touches the soul. Select a song, a poem, or a piece of art, literature, or film that relates to this card. Describe its relevance.

Mandala

In Chapter 4, you will create a personal tarot mandala. Select an image that exemplifies this card. Take a photograph or draw a picture. Choose an existing photo, a magazine picture, or an item that personally illustrates the card to you.

VIII. Strength

Description

A beautiful woman, dressed in white and garlanded with flowers, stands over a lion. Above her head is the infinity symbol and around her is the magnificence of nature. She holds in her hands the mouth of a ferocious beast, yet her face shows no strain. Her gentle strength is spiritual in nature. Her purity and spiritual force easily subdue the passion and emotional energy of the lion.[10] She is the feminine warrior who expresses love as her greatest strength.

Self-Exploration

1. Look at the card and note how it makes you feel. Do you like this character?

2. One of the most feminine types of strength is endurance. Contemplate endurance and describe an experience when you were able to "go the distance."

3. Love makes difficult things possible. That is why the lady in the Strength card can hold open the mouth of the lion effortlessly. Remember a time when approaching a difficult task with an attitude of love made it possible to achieve your task.

4. Sometimes we have to do things that we know are best for ourselves and those we love, yet we don't know if we possess the strength to follow through. While contemplating the Strength card, choose something you've been afraid to face, and resolve to gather the strength to eloquently accomplish your goal.

5. Western culture places great emphasis on the power of action and dynamic force, of masculine strength. However, as balanced individuals, we also need to understand our natural ability to wield

the type of feminine strength that this mentor illustrates. Name four ways in which you can incorporate gentle, feminine strength into your life. An example might be to reach out to people who need your assistance and contribute to their well-being in some way. This action would relate even more specifically to the message of the Strength mentor if you are in some way fearful of the process. An example might be helping the homeless, handicapped, elderly or terminally ill, even if you are not comfortable in those situations. I'm sure Mother Teresa found the streets of Calcutta extremely frightening the first time she picked up a dying person and lovingly cared for him. Nevertheless, she infused her heart with love and continued to demonstrate feminine strength to every person she picked up thereafter.

Affirmation

Our beliefs create our reality. Write a personal affirmation that reflects your beliefs seen through the mirror of this major mentor. I have provided one for you.

My greatest strength comes from a loving heart.

Action

You have explored your thoughts and feelings by answering the questions above. This has been your inner work. Now, as part of your outer work, take some action! Perform an activity, action, or ritual that relates to the lessons of this card. It will help you to fully experience the message of the card as well as the aspect of yourself represented by the archetype. I have provided some examples. After completing the task, note your observations.

- Face a difficult or hostile situation with a loving heart rather than with fear.
- Do something to help someone in need without him/her knowing it was you. Don't take any credit for your anonymous assistance.
- Tackle something you've been afraid to face. If you have a paralyzing fear or phobia, resolve to rid yourself of it through whatever mode of therapy is appropriate for you. Make immediate arrangements to meet with someone who can help you. Melt your fear with a loving

heart, and love yourself enough to take action today.

Art

Art touches the soul. Select a song, a poem, or a piece of art, literature, or film that relates to this card. Describe its relevance.

Mandala

In Chapter 4, you will create a personal tarot mandala. Select an image that exemplifies this card. Take a photograph or draw a picture. Choose an existing photo, a magazine picture, or an item that personally illustrates the card to you.

IX. The Hermit

Description

A solitary monk stands upon a snowy mountain peak. The mountain represents heightened consciousness. In one of the monk's hands is a lantern containing the shining star of consciousness, while the other holds the staff of intuition. His light shows the way to all who dare follow him, but the path is treacherous. The wise Hermit in this illustration transcended the physical realm and is no longer a man of this world. It is said that, because of this, "his loneliness is vast beyond belief, and glorious beyond all imagination."[11]

Self-Exploration

1. Look at the card and note how it makes you feel. Do you like this character?

2. Recollect a time when you chose or were forced by circumstances to be alone and derived healing and/or clarity from the experience.

3. In what aspect of your life do you currently feel that you are "on your own," with only your heart and mind to guide you?

4. Silence, meditation, and reflection are like food for the soul. Is there some time in your daily life that you can designate for this spiritual practice? If you were to turn within and simply listen, what do you think your Higher Self or Higher Power would tell you?

5. It is said that we come into this world alone and move onto the next world alone. What do you find appealing about being alone? What do you fear about being alone?

Affirmation

Our beliefs create our reality. Write a personal affirmation that reflects your beliefs seen through the mirror of this major mentor. I have provided one for you.

The light of the Divine shines within me, illuminating my path.

Action

You have explored your thoughts and feelings by answering the questions above. This has been your inner work. Now, as part of your outer work, take some action! Perform an activity, action, or ritual that relates to the lessons of this card. It will help you to fully experience the message of the card as well as the aspect of yourself represented by the archetype. I have provided some examples. After completing the task, note your observations.

- Concentrate on the light of a candle, like the Hermit's lantern. After a while, close your eyes and feel your inner light radiating.
- Concentrate, contemplate, and meditate. Pray. Turn within.
- Take some time to be completely alone. Take a personal retreat in whatever manner suits you.
- Reach out to someone who is completely alone.

Art

Art touches the soul. Select a song, a poem, or a piece of art, literature, or film that relates to this card. Describe its relevance.

Mandala

In Chapter 4, you will create a personal tarot mandala. Select an image that exemplifies this card. Take a photograph or draw a picture. Choose an existing photo, a magazine picture, or an item that personally illustrates the card to you.

WHEEL of FORTUNE.

X. Wheel of Fortune

Description

Symbols of the four elements hover on clouds around a great wheel. These are the angels or "apocalyptic beasts" of Ezekiel's vision from the Bible's Old Testament. Figures ascend and descend as the wheel turns, while a sphinx holding the sword of truth sits regally atop the wheel in the position of central balance. The alchemical symbols and Hebrew letters adorning the Wheel represent the soul's transformation within the ever-moving, ever-changing process that is symbolized in the illustration. Worldly fortune is depicted as transient at best, while the eternal soul remains steadfast.

Self Exploration

1. Look at the card and note how it makes you feel. Do you like this image?
2. "What goes up must come down" is an adage that corresponds well to the lessons of the Wheel of Fortune card. When we are down on the wheel of life, we can take comfort in the knowledge that the only way left for the wheel to turn is up. Conversely, when we are up on the wheel and everything we touch seems to figuratively turn to gold, it is important to remember that the Wheel of Fortune is dynamic and ever-turning. If we place too much importance on our good fortune, we may find that it is merely transitory. Look at the sphinx in the illustration as representing those people who have remained constant throughout life's changes. Who and what have you been able to count on at every stage of your life? What has remained constant and unchanging when everything around you was in a state of flux and change?

3. Good luck, good fortune, and success are often attributed to this card. If you suddenly came into a great fortune, what would you do with your wealth? What new ventures would you explore? And in what way would this success or good fortune transform you or your world?

4. The sphinx who remains steady atop the Wheel of Fortune appears to be a Buddha-like figure who finds his truth in the point of equilibrium. Throughout life's ups and downs, this character remains focused on the middle way, rather than becoming overly affected by highs and lows. Is there a situation (or relationship) in your life today that pulls you up and down? Could this situation be handled more effectively by approaching it from a more detached frame of reference?

5. The alchemical symbols around the Wheel of Fortune represent the sometimes painful process of transformation which refines us toward our highest potentiality. Reflect upon some of life's more difficult lessons and describe how these experiences have helped to create the person you are today.

Affirmation

Our beliefs create our reality. Write a personal affirmation that reflects your beliefs seen through the mirror of this major mentor. I have provided one for you.

My greatest, everlasting wealth is measured by the fullness of my heart.

Action

You have explored your thoughts and feelings by answering the questions above. This has been your inner work. Now, as part of your outer work, take some action! Perform an activity, action, or ritual that relates to the lessons of this card. It will help you to fully experience the message of the card as well as the aspect of yourself represented by the archetype. I have provided some examples. After completing the task, note your observations.

- Take a risk in the workplace.
- Give something of yours away—position, money, stuff. You can't take it with you.

- Find a way to thank three people who have remained constant throughout life's ups and downs. Let them know how much you appreciate their steadfastness.
- As a liberating experience, select something that represents an impoverished period in your life as well as something that represents a prosperous period in your life. Display these items together in a place where you can look at them and reflect on impermanence.

Art

Art touches the soul. Select a song, a poem, or a piece of art, literature, or film that relates to this card. Describe its relevance.

Mandala

In Chapter 4, you will create a personal tarot mandala. Select an image that exemplifies this card. Take a photograph or draw a picture. Choose an existing photo, a magazine picture, or an item that personally illustrates the card to you.

XI. Justice

Description

The Lady of Justice sits in a position of balance between two pillars of polar opposites. Her eyes are unveiled because she represents Divine Justice, rather than human justice, which is blind.

She holds the sword of truth, which can be wielded severely, although the scales in her left hand indicate fairness and balanced judgment. Everything is ultimately revealed to the open eyes of the figure who raises the powerful sword of karmic righteousness.

Self-Exploration

1. Look at the card and note how it makes you feel. Do you like this character?

2. The expression, "what goes around comes around" defines an important belief regarding the nature of things. Consider the Christian teachings, "As you sow, so shall you reap," "Do unto others what you would like them to do unto you," and "What you do to the least of my brothers, that you do unto me." These teachings, as well as the three-fold law of Wicca and the Hindu law of karma all express the same admonishment: whatever you put out into the universe will eventually come back to you. This is the law of justice. Describe some "seeds" you have planted in the past which eventually grew and bore fruit. What seeds have you recently planted?

3. Divine justice bears open eyes because the Divine knows fully what is in our hearts and in our minds. We are often blindfolded to the details of a situation and experience it only from our limited point of view. Do you believe in Divine fairness and the natural order of things? Do you trust that justice will ultimately be served? Remember

a time when you experienced something that, at the time, seemed unfair or didn't make sense but, in retrospect, was clearly for the best. Then, consider something that recently has been difficult to accept, doesn't seem fair, or just doesn't make sense to you. Can you proclaim to yourself that you trust in Divine justice? Do you also trust that clarity regarding this situation will be yours in due time?

4. The Justice card teaches us to use impartial judgment and a balanced intellect when making a decision. Is there a decision that needs to be made in your life that requires clarity of mind? How can the formidable image of the Lady of Justice, with her sword of truth raised high, assist or inspire you in making your decision?

5. The law of karma teaches us that we cannot run from life's experiences or lessons. Clearly, if we avoid the lessons that are presented to us, we only delay the inevitable, and will be presented even more powerful lessons in the future. Describe a lesson that you tried to avoid learning and which returned until you understood the message loudly and clearly.

Affirmation

Our beliefs create our reality. Write a personal affirmation that reflects your beliefs seen through the mirror of this major mentor. I have provided one for you.

I believe in Divine justice and the order of the universe.

Action

You have explored your thoughts and feelings by answering the questions above. This has been your inner work. Now, as part of your outer work, take some action! Perform an activity, action, or ritual that relates to the lessons of this card. It will help you to fully experience the message of the card as well as the aspect of yourself represented by the archetype. I have provided some examples. After completing the task, note your observations.

• Consider a situation about which you are harboring sadness or resentment. Choose something that does not or did not seem fair. Write down the details of the situation and express your resentment on one side of a piece of paper. On the other side, affirm your belief in the law of Divine justice and commit to letting go of your resentment. Bury the paper in a garden, like a seed of forgiveness, which will later bear the fruit of healing. Plant a flower there if you wish.

• Intentionally put something good out into the universe. Plant some karmic seeds that will later grow and bear fruit. Keep in mind that what you put out will eventually come back to you, but not always in the way you expect.

Art

Art touches the soul. Select a song, a poem, or a piece of art, literature, or film that relates to this card. Describe its relevance.

Mandala

In Chapter 4, you will create a personal tarot mandala. Select an image that exemplifies this card. Take a photograph or draw a picture. Choose an existing photo, a magazine picture, or an item that personally illustrates the card to you.

XII. The Hanged Man

Description

A man hangs upside-down from one leg, suspended on a living, t-shaped tree. His bent leg helps to shape the number four, which is a number of completion. His face is tranquil and brightly illuminated, despite his compromised position. His hands are behind his back, suggesting a state of serenity and repose. Some believe that there is a relationship between this card and the Christian Apostle, Peter. It is said that Peter asked to be crucified in a manner that was different than Jesus as a sign of humility and respect for his Lord.

Self-Exploration

1. Look at the card and note how it makes you feel. Do you like this character?

2. The Hanged Man represents time in suspension. The character is taking a pause in his life, "hanging out," so to speak, in order to avail himself of higher wisdom. He is in a state of repose as he waits to take the next spiritual step. Our culture glorifies action and dynamism. It constantly urges us to strive, to work harder, and to push forward. However, what we often need to do is to simply wait. There is a proper time for everything, and "being" must balance "doing" in order for us to create harmony in our lives and in ourselves. What aspect of your spiritual journey would now be best served by "being" rather than "doing," by waiting rather than working?

3. The Hanged Man is upside down, in a position that is contrary to the natural order of things. This unique position offers him an equally unique perspective. In fact, he sees things in a whole new way. Is there a current situation or condition in your life that needs to be

viewed from a different angle? Perhaps there are new and innovative ideas waiting to be realized. Remember a time when addressing someone or something from a new perspective afforded you the revelation or "aha!" that you needed in order to proceed.

4. We often attain our greatest wisdom through sacrifice. The spiritual experience of the Hanged Man card also relates to repentance, self-sacrifice, and the suspension of the will to gain something of much greater value. Consider someone you admire who voluntarily made a sacrifice in order to attain wisdom or knowledge of a spiritual nature. Have you had a similar experience? Is this a lesson that is relevant to you in your life today? Think about what you are and are not willing to give up in order to attain your spiritual goals.

5. The Hanged Man's body creates the outline of the number four, which is a number of completion. The Hanged Man card is a transition card, indicating a turning point or a readiness for change. Some refer to it as a sort of initiation or baptism card, one that represents consciousness opening to inner truth. What have you completed on one level and are prepared to begin on a new higher level? In what area of your life have you reached such a turning point and feel the readiness and willingness described above?

Affirmation

Our beliefs create our reality. Write a personal affirmation that reflects your beliefs seen through the mirror of this major mentor. I have provided one for you.

My eyes are open to new perspectives; I am ready to move to the next level.

Action

You have explored your thoughts and feelings by answering the questions above. This has been your inner work. Now, as part of your outer work, take some action! Perform an activity, action, or ritual that relates to the lessons of this card. It will help you to fully experience the message of the card as well as the aspect of yourself represented by the archetype. I have provided some examples. After completing the task, note your observations.

- Do as many things differently as you can in one day in order to gain a new perspective. For example, go to work a different way or choose a different mode of transportation. Take your lunch break at a different time, in a different place, and eat something completely different. Wear different clothes or different colors than you are used to, etc. If it's your day off, do something completely different than usual.
- Handle a situation in a completely different manner than is usual for you. If this situation involves other people, pay special attention to the ways in which they are affected by your changed behavior. In what ways are you affected by "stretching" out of your comfort zone?
- Make a sacrifice for the greater good—for your family, for your community, even for your own well-being.

Art

Art touches the soul. Select a song, a poem, or a piece of art, literature, or film that relates to this card. Describe its relevance.

Mandala

In Chapter 4, you will create a personal tarot mandala. Select an image that exemplifies this card. Take a photograph or draw a picture. Choose an existing photo, a magazine picture, or an item that personally illustrates the card to you.

XIII. Death

Description

An armor-clad skeleton rides through a landscape where he encounters four people of various ages. Each represents one of the four primary stations or classes within medieval society (clergy, royalty, merchant, and peasant). The horse is white, indicating the purity of the rider's functions as creator of closure and bringer of change. The skeleton of death holds a flag displaying a rose. The rose symbolizes the heart and the full flowering/unfolding of the self. It is through the heart, or love, that we realize our highest potential. In the background, a boat sails through the river of life, indicating the journey through consciousness. The sun rising between two pillars in the distance illustrates the new birth which inevitably follows death.

Self-Exploration

1. Look at the card and note how it makes you feel. Do you like this illustration?
2. The death card is the primary "change" mentor of the tarot. By embracing the many little deaths of life, we embrace change and, thus, the possibility of rebirth/renewal. It takes an enormous amount of strength and courage to face death and let go. What are you having difficulty letting go of, and what life changes are you currently resisting?
3. The glory of day precedes the dark of night, just as the magnificence of spring always follows the "dead" of winter. These metaphors from the natural world help to bring us hope when we are experiencing an emotional or spiritual "dark night of the soul." Describe an experience when you have faced such a dark night. Reflect on your

journey out of that darkness.

4. The death card is the most "democratic" of all the tarot's mentors because no person, regardless of social standing or power, can avoid its inevitability. Moreover, the process of change, of death, and of loss helps to shape us and recreate our beliefs. Contemplate loss, and name seven things (large or small) that you have lost in your lifetime. Note how these experiences have helped to mold you into the person you are today. Especially, how have you ultimately benefitted from your loss?

5. The mythical Phoenix rises from its own ashes; the humble caterpillar transforms itself into the butterfly in all its splendor. A stagnant pool dies, while a moving river yields new life. Indeed, "transform or die" should be our daily motto. What are you now willing to give up in order to become the person you want to be, to realize your own potential and spiritual goals?

Affirmation

Our beliefs create our reality. Write a personal affirmation that reflects your beliefs seen through the mirror of this major mentor. I have provided one for you.

I invite change because I am willing to let go of who I am to embrace the person I can become.

Action

You have explored your thoughts and feelings by answering the questions above. This has been your inner work. Now, as part of your outer work, take some action! Perform an activity, action, or ritual that relates to the lessons of this card. It will help you to fully experience the message of the card as well as the aspect of yourself represented by the archetype. I have provided some examples. After completing the task, note your observations.

- Let go of something. Like the grim reaper with his scythe, cut something out of your life that has reached its natural conclusion and is ready to rest in peace. Mourn its passing, if that is helpful, then move on. Rebirth always follows death.

- Visit an art museum or gallery and pay special attention to artwork that represents death, winter, or closure to you. Immerse yourself in its unique beauty and powerful message.

- If the season is winter, take some time to experience nature and contemplate the profundity of the natural process. If it is not winter, visit a stark landscape (such as a desert, a city, or a rocky area without vegetation) and contemplate the subtleties of this harsh terrain.

Art

Art touches the soul. Select a song, a poem, or a piece of art, literature, or film that relates to this card. Describe its relevance.

Mandala

In Chapter 4, you will create a personal tarot mandala. Select an image that exemplifies this card. Take a photograph or draw a picture. Choose an existing photo, a magazine picture, or an item that personally illustrates the card to you.

XIV. Temperance

Description

With one foot on land and the other in water, the Archangel Michael pours a liquid substance from one vessel to another. This mixing process represents the inner alchemy of purification, transmutation, and co-creation. The angel's countenance suggests a state of inner balance and harmony. Flowers grow beside him, depicting the beauty of nature, while beyond him lies a radiant path leading toward a brilliant sunrise. The triangle on Michael's gown indicates fire in the heart and soul, yet the dynamic force is carefully grounded—focused on the supreme goal.

Self-Exploration

1. Look at the card and note how it makes you feel. Do you like this character?
2. The original meaning of temperance relates to cutting wine with water, moderation, economy, frugality, and discipline. It relates to graciously taking less, rather than greedily wanting more. Consider how excess and addiction run rampant in our modern culture. Truly, we work too hard, we eat too much (or, in some cases, too unhealthily or too little). We may even use drugs, alcohol, and medications to help us cope with the demands of our chosen lifestyle. The Temperance mentor is beautiful, but it is neither wishy-washy nor ambivalent. The image's main character is Michael, a fiery, powerful Archangel who is illustrated directing his energy purposefully. We all know that it requires much more power and strength to say no to excess than to indulge ourselves. Consider your own excesses, your own extremes, and resolve to moderate yourself

in the best interests of your spiritual growth and your own supreme goal. Note your thoughts on paper.

3. There is a grounded place between intellect and emotion, between passivity and dynamism, between yin and yang. It is the middle way. Buddhism advocates this middle way of tolerance and temperance, of serenity and balance, of harmony and inner peace. Divine Illumination can be found in such a place of inner tranquillity. Name ten things that you do to create a peaceful state within you. Perhaps you immerse yourself in prayer or ritual. You may listen to music or take candle-lit baths or become swept away by the splendor of nature. You might involve yourself in a community of like-minded individuals who support your spiritual quest. If you cannot list ten, add some things you could be doing if you took the time and effort to do so.

4. The tasks of bridge-building and creating harmony within relationships relate to the powerful message of the Temperance card. Contemplate the following list of words/concepts. Note what feelings or thoughts come to mind with each word:
   - combination
   - coordination
   - partnership
   - teamwork
   - adaptation
   - weaving
   - flowing
   - harmonizing

5. The Temperance card is a healing card. Through purification, the release of the ego, and our will focused on the Divine, we come to a place where the past flows through the present and the future. Our energy is able to flow freely, in concert with the universal pulse of life. Through this Divine conduit, we can achieve the power of healing, of art, and of co-creation. Describe the following life experiences:
   - You provided healing to someone.
   - Someone provided healing to you.

- You created something from deep within yourself—the essence of true "art."

Affirmation

Our beliefs create our reality. Write a personal affirmation that reflects your beliefs seen through the mirror of this major mentor. I have provided one for you.

I walk the middle path of inner balance and serenity.

Action

You have explored your thoughts and feelings by answering the questions above. This has been your inner work. Now, as part of your outer work, take some action! Perform an activity, action, or ritual that relates to the lessons of this card. It will help you to fully experience the message of the card as well as the aspect of yourself represented by the archetype. I have provided some examples. After completing the task, note your observations.

- Visit a very noisy, busy place (airport, shopping mall, etc.) and sit. Pay attention to your breathing and consciously alter your consciousness to a point where you feel relaxed and peaceful. Remain acutely aware of what is going on, while remaining detached and at ease. Don't block out the noise and activity. Rather, use it as a sort of mantra to ease you into a state of heightened awareness. Note your observations.

- Take action and remove from your home and workplace those items that you have trouble using moderately (e.g., alcohol, drugs, unhealthy foods, etc.) Resolve to take steps toward removing addiction and excess from your life. This may be one of the most important actions you will ever take in your life, so seek all the help and support you need.

- Do something that is intensely creative—something you love. Your result will be art in its truest form. Use a medium you are comfortable with, or try something new. Let go of expectation about the result. Instead, flow with the process of creating. Write a poem, a story, a letter, or a song. Paint a picture, build, carve, or stitch. Create a masterpiece in the kitchen or interpret your being through dance.

The sky is the limit.
- In one day, do at least three things that are meditative. You could meditate in the morning, give thanks at your meals, and take a candle-lit bath with gentle background music in the evening. Pay attention to the way in which your state of well-being is enhanced by integrating serenity into your daily life.

Art

Art touches the soul. Select a song, a poem, or a piece of art, literature, or film that relates to this card. Describe its relevance.

Mandala

In Chapter 4, you will create a personal tarot mandala. Select an image that exemplifies this card. Take a photograph or draw a picture. Choose an existing photo, a magazine picture, or an item that personally illustrates the card to you.

XV. The Devil

Description

A huge figure of a winged devil, depicted as a half-man, half-goat, perches on a black platform. This character is made to resemble Pan or Dionysis, relating to instinctive behavior and animal passions. Judeo-Christian beliefs introduced society to the character named Satan who reigns in evil opposition to God. However, ancient Goddess-worshipping cultures did not share such a belief. The "pagans" of old saw Pan as a personification of fertility, passion and life force, not of evil. It is important to understand that this character in our tarot illustration is a product of Judeo-Christian beliefs only and has no association with earth-based religions like Wicca.

Two servants, a man and a woman, stand before the Devil wearing horns and tails. The Devil, in its Judeo-Christian interpretation, is androgynous (neither male nor female) and represents the state of farthest extreme from God. The servants are clothed only with chains, but the chains around their necks are loose enough to remove easily. The loose chains illustrate attachments that are created by our own choices and can be broken by employing free will. The Devil holds one hand up, showing the sign of Saturn on his palm (restriction), while his other hand holds an inverted torch (destruction). Atop the card is an inverted pentagram, indicating the Devil's emphasis on the elements of fire and earth (power and the material world). This is in opposition to the traditional, upward-pointing pentagram, which emphasizes spirit or God as reigning supreme over the other four elements.

Self-Exploration

1. Look at the card and note how it makes you feel. Do you like these characters?

2. The Devil card always relates to blocks. It is a card of restriction, of limitations, of rigidity. In fact, the Devil's real power comes from suppressed love. When love flows, it creates healing; when it is blocked, it creates hate and, eventually, destruction. Like the servants in the illustration, we create our own prisons or servitude through our negative beliefs and selfish choices. By removing the chains of rigidity and limiting beliefs, we are free to once again be infused by the healing light of the Divine. Reflect on the following questions and note your responses:

   • What beliefs hold you captive and how do you intend to break free from the weight of limitation and restriction?

   • Are you withholding love? How do you intend to break free from the destructive force of this suppression?

   • It is said that where there is light, there can be no darkness. Hence, our fears must be faced, or we give them the power to destroy us. Is there a fear that paralyzes you? How do you intend to break free from its powerful grip?

3. The Devil's pentagram points downward, placing disproportionate emphasis on power and materialism. Truly, one of our greatest temptations is to become shackled to material attachments like power, money, status, and success. We need to have control over these things, rather than be controlled by them. It is easy to become a prisoner to our possessions and find ourselves cleaving to things that are empty of love and life. It is crucial that we regularly evaluate the lives and value structures we have adopted for ourselves. What material attachments are you chained to and in what ways can you loosen your shackles? Are you placing disproportionate emphasis on the wrong "points" of the pentagram? Which way does your personal pentagram point?

4. We all have the capacity for evil. Whenever we lose sight of our Divine birthright, we invite our "negative" natures to flourish. When we lose sight of our spiritual goals, it becomes easy to use fate or

circumstance as an excuse for not taking responsibility for our actions. We then weaken our resolve and allow others to control our lives. In what ways and in what areas can you regain control of your life and return your focus to the Divine?

5. Becoming whole isn't about removing every negative aspect of our personalities and becoming completely pure. It's about owning our selves in our entirety and endeavoring to channel even our negative characteristics in positive ways. As an archetype, the Devil represents our shadow natures. If you were to boldly face your shadow self, what characteristics could you redirect to help you achieve your spiritual goals? For example, perhaps one could redirect intense ambition toward spiritual attainment with the right goals, awareness, and focus. After identifying the characteristics, describe your plan to enact this process.

Affirmation

Our beliefs create our reality. Write a personal affirmation that reflects your beliefs seen through the mirror of this major mentor. I have provided one for you.

I now choose to break free from the prisons I have created and allow love to flow through me.

Action

You have explored your thoughts and feelings by answering the questions above. This has been your inner work. Now, as part of your outer work, take some action! Perform an activity, action, or ritual that relates to the lessons of this card. It will help you to fully experience the message of the card as well as the aspect of yourself represented by the archetype. I have provided some examples. After completing the task, note your observations.

• Symbolically break through a barrier that you have consciously or unconsciously created for yourself. Write it on a board and break it. Write it on a plate and smash it. Shout it from the rooftop. Find an effective way to express this breakthrough. Remember, you created it. You can break through it.

- Renounce something (or someone) in your life that has an unwanted hold over you. Remove the shackles and take control of your own life.
- Look a block, obstacle, or fear straight in the eye and then force it to crumble. Take steps to relinquish its power over you, using whatever method or support is appropriate for you.

Art

Art touches the soul. Select a song, a poem, or a piece of art, literature, or film that relates to this card. Describe its relevance.

Mandala

In Chapter 4, you will create a personal tarot mandala. Select an image that exemplifies this card. Take a photograph or draw a picture. Choose an existing photo, a magazine picture, or an item that personally illustrates the card to you.

THE TOWER.

XVI. The Tower

Description

Out of the night sky comes a flash of lightning, blasting away a crown from the top of a tower. Two people are seen falling from the structure to their inevitable deaths. Fire blazes inside the tower and hailstones, depicted as yods, fill the sky. (Yods are Hebrew letters, indicating the Divine origin of the fire.) Traditionally, the Tower mentor is associated with the Tower of Babel from the Bible's Old Testament, which was often illustrated by medieval artists. The Tower in this illustration has been built on barren rock and represents a tower of earthly attachments or a house of false doctrine/beliefs.[12] It is a structure built by misplaced effort and stands in the way of what is truly real. The Divine lightning bolt of the Higher Self causes the edifice to crumble, leaving only truth in its wake.

Self-Exploration

1. Look at the card and note how it makes you feel. Do you like this image?
2. What "false gods" have you erected towers to? Have you placed all of your time, effort, heart, and resources into your work, your outward appearance, or your social standing? The Tower card teaches us that any false securities that we have built around us will be blasted away as a sort of spiritual purification. All illusion will be shattered and purged when we travel earnestly down the road to Divine awakening. This process teaches us that the things we considered permanent in our lives are easily lost. Consider what beliefs, habits, or values no longer serve you. Write a former, outmoded belief in the form of an affirmation. Briefly describe why it no longer serves you.

Then, write a new affirmation that better suits your renewed spiritual goals. (Example: Old belief: "I'm too busy to meditate." This belief no longer serves me because it is not helping me achieve my goal of oneness with the Divine. New belief: "I have time each and every day for meditation because spiritual attainment is the highest priority in my life.")

3. When everything around you is in shambles, it's like cleaning a closet. At the point of overwhelm, when you've taken everything out of the closet and have a huge mess in front of you, it's tempting to give up. You yearn to put everything back into the closet and close the door. It seems like it would be easier to do that than to go through every item, evaluate its usefulness, and purge. The inner cleansing process is similar to closet cleaning because things often seem to get much worse before they get better. Radical change and turmoil can be unpleasant, but such powerful forces can be extremely cathartic and effective in shaking up our consciousness.

   The Hindu System of yoga encourages the destruction of pride and illusion. It depicts the Goddess Kali as the destroyer of falsehood, a shatterer of old forms that prevent us from embracing truth. In the aftermath of the cataclysm, there comes a radical shift in which the spiritual centers awaken. We achieve the flash of illumination and, ultimately, experience utter clarity. The profound catharsis brings a new birth—a sort of baptism by fire. What inner closets do you need to clean? Perhaps there are pent-up feelings you need to purge or memories that need to be dredged and released. Consider the merit of this process and resolve to begin the messy work of digging in and shaking things up in order to clear the sacred space inside of you.

4. When tragedy strikes, epiphany or illumination sometimes follows. Many people who have experienced the sudden loss of (or access to) their material possessions—through fire, flood, or theft for example—also have experienced a profound sense of clarity when they realize how many "things" they could comfortably live without. Do you remember a time when you wiped your slate clean and started fresh? If not, is there someone else who you have admired for starting anew? (This could be someone from your life or, if no such person exists, from history or even fiction.)

5. What are your ten most important values? Take time to reflect on why they are so meaningful to you.

Affirmation

Our beliefs create our reality. Write a personal affirmation that reflects your beliefs seen through the mirror of this major mentor. I have provided one for you.

I focus only on Truth as I renounce falsity and illusion.

Action

You have explored your thoughts and feelings by answering the questions above. This has been your inner work. Now, as part of your outer work, take some action! Perform an activity, action, or ritual that relates to the lessons of this card. It will help you to fully experience the message of the card as well as the aspect of yourself represented by the archetype. I have provided some examples. After completing the task, note your observations.

- Write down any old beliefs that are no longer useful to you. Write them on some specially chosen paper and symbolically burn them. Place new affirmations in key locations around your house to reinforce your new beliefs.

- Through books, documentaries, or the internet, explore the process of natural disasters such as the eruption of volcanos. After the cataclysm has subsided, how does the earth heal? In what ways does nature utilize disaster for the purposes of creation? In the Australian outback, there are plants and flowers that require the intense heat of bush fires in order to grow. After the eruption of Washington's Mt. St. Helens, people thought the surrounding landscape would be forever barren, yet life returned. The study of these natural processes could be very insightful for you.

- Purge your stuff. Sift through your material possessions and get rid of excess clutter. Lighten your load.

Art

Art touches the soul. Select a song, a poem, or a piece of art, literature, or film that relates to this card. Describe its relevance.

Mandala

In Chapter 4, you will create a personal tarot mandala. Select an image that exemplifies this card. Take a photograph or draw a picture. Choose an existing photo, a magazine picture, or an item that personally illustrates the card to you.

XVII. The Star

Description

A lovely, naked woman kneels by a pool of water. She places one foot in the water, and rests the other foot on land. Water pours freely from two pitchers, indicating emotions and the depth of consciousness. As the water nourishes the land, hopes and dreams are manifested on the material plane. Flowers, illustrating the beauty of creation, grow around the central figure, while an ibis bird, symbolizing natural intelligence and inner wisdom, perches on the tree of knowledge. The large yellow star above the woman's head represents her aim or goal; the small white stars represent the collective unconscious. This is a glorious, spiritual card describing hope and the immortal soul as well as the gift of Divine grace.

Self-Exploration

1. Look at the card and note how it makes you feel. Do you like this character?

2. The central figure in the Star card is sometimes attributed to Aquarius, the water bearer, who nourishes with compassion, charity, and humanitarian service. Like barren earth, there are many situations in the world around us that are dry and lifeless—areas greatly in need of replenishment. The Star card speaks of the power of hope and encouragement. When we begin the cycle of encouragement by giving hope to others, we receive hope ourselves and, in turn, elevate the universal consciousness. In what ways do you nourish the world around you? Is there a noble cause you would like to infuse with your life force?

3. The Star has been called "the calm after the storm" ("storm"

referring to the destructive force of the previous mentor, the Tower). There is a deep cleansing that the Star promises, a healing energy that soothes and reinforces us after we have been shaken. When contemplating the Star, we must contemplate the manner in which we express our emotions. When we hold our emotions back, and contain our deepest feelings safely and comfortably, we risk becoming numb. But when we dare to feel, we open the door to truth and the depth of understanding. It is essential, though, that we surround ourselves with a positive support system when we reach out to share ourselves. We need a nurturing group, family or at least one trusted person to share our hopes, fears, ideas, and inspirations. This deep sharing process provides healing to everyone involved. Describe your emotional support system and the people with whom you share your deepest feelings.

4. The star above the woman's head in this tarot card is said to represent her most profound goal. Without goals to focus our efforts, we wander aimlessly and haphazardly through life. The woman in the illustration pours water onto the land, symbolizing ideas made manifest here on earth. What are your four most important goals? Write them down and evaluate them each from various angles: What is the purpose of your goal? In what way will it enrich your life as well as the lives of others? Is it stagnant or expansive? A stagnant goal is one in which there is no higher purpose. An expansive goal will yield rewards because it remains ever open to new possibilities.

5. The Star is an extremely spiritual card. It symbolizes the immortal soul or the Divine within. When we dwell within a meditative state, we open ourselves to spiritual insight and clarity of vision. We connect with our Higher Selves/Holy Spirit/Atman. We are filled with grace and, for a brief moment, truth is unveiled. Describe a time when you have had a peak experience—when you felt connected with the universal oneness and, even briefly, experienced Divine grace.

Affirmation

Our beliefs create our reality. Write a personal affirmation that reflects your beliefs seen through the mirror of this major mentor. I have provided one for you.

I am bathed clean in the healing waters of hope. I am one with the Divine.

Action

You have explored your thoughts and feelings by answering the questions above. This has been your inner work. Now, as part of your outer work, take some action! Perform an activity, action, or ritual that relates to the lessons of this card. It will help you to fully experience the message of the card as well as the aspect of yourself represented by the archetype. I have provided some examples. After completing the task, note your observations.

- Do some goal-setting. Write down your goals, then post them in a location where you can review them daily.
- Call someone or send a note to give hope and encouragement.
- Bring water to a dry location and symbolically water the earth, providing nourishment.
- Let go of a situation that you believe is "hopeless" and release it into the hands of the Divine/the Universe. Faith and trust is the key here.

Art

Art touches the soul. Select a song, a poem, or a piece of art, literature, or film that relates to this card. Describe its relevance.

Mandala

In Chapter 4, you will create a personal tarot mandala. Select an image that exemplifies this card. Take a photograph or draw a picture. Choose an existing photo, a magazine picture, or an item that personally illustrates the card to you.

XVIII. The Moon

Description

The moon in its three phases shines brightly over a nocturnal landscape. A woman in the moon looks down on the creatures below, observing the manner in which they are affected by her lunar powers. A lobster rises from a tidal pool, symbolizing the soul's ascent through the unconscious. The path ahead of the creature leads to illumination and rebirth, and bypasses two imposing structures on its evolutionary journey. These towers are sometimes attributed to our defenses, sometimes to our fears, illustrating that what is hidden in darkness (the dark places within ourselves) must be revealed into the light before we reach the summit of attainment. A wolf and a dog howl at the moon, representing the wild and domesticated aspects of our instinctual natures.[13] The yods emanating from the moon indicate the Divine life-force which vitalizes and fortifies the emotional self.

Self-Exploration

1. Look at the card and note how it makes you feel. Do you like this image?

2. The Moon card sometimes warns of hidden enemies or dangers, of forces we can't see clearly in the darkness. The most powerful tool we have in our feminine aspects (men have feminine aspects as well as women) is our lunar natures. When we affirm the validity of our intuition or "gut-level feelings," that trust enables us to regain our ability to see into the darkness. Recount an experience when you were faced with deception or danger because you chose to ignore your intuition.

3. The Moon card represents the ancient mysteries and the descent

into the subconscious mind. In the distant past, seekers were initiated into the mysteries through powerful rituals that altered their states of consciousness. Today, we use other means to create shifts in our awareness. We use constructive tools such as meditation and prayer, art and dreams, lovemaking and physical endurance as well as destructive tools like drugs and alcohol—all to propel us inward. Because the spiritual journey requires deep inward exploration, it is to our benefit that we begin a dialogue with our subconscious mind. One of the most effective ways to do this is to pay close attention to our dreams. What does your subconscious want to say to you? Make a list of symbols that you remembered from your recent dreams. Interpret them—intuitively or with the help of a dream interpretation book. (Don't be overly concerned if the interpretations don't immediately make sense.) Then, place a pad and pen next to your bed and resolve to make recording and interpreting your future dreams a daily practice.

4. It is said that the moon effects the fluids within our bodies, and clearly, we are made up of mostly water. Perhaps the water in our brains responds like the tides, ebbing and flowing with the force of subconscious lunar magnetism. We can all share stories of how "crazy" things can be when the moon is full, how hospitals see more accidents and mental institutions experience more difficulty. The Moon card invites us to immerse ourselves in our shadow selves and acknowledge our more unawakened primitive natures. Honestly and without judgment, reflect upon some of the more negative aspects of your nature. Reflect upon an experience when you acted or made a judgment without being fully informed or by being in some way unaware. Using the metaphor of light and darkness, you acted without having sufficient light. After sufficient light was shed on the situation, perhaps you learned that you attacked an illusion rather than a truth. In what way did this or other situations like it provide a learning experience for you? These kinds of lessons are part of the experience of the Moon mentor.

5. First question for a male reader: Like the proverbial light at the end of the tunnel, the moon illuminates our paths through the dark of night. Recollect a time when you traversed a dangerous path or

experienced an emotionally dark time. What light shone for you, enabling you to see through the darkness? Describe the events and, especially, the feelings associated with that experience.

Second question for a female reader: The Moon card illustrates the moon in its full splendor—in all three aspects—representing the three distinct levels of women's experience—maiden, mother, and crone. Celebrating the mysteries of womanhood, in all of her distinct aspects, is part of claiming the richness of our spiritual natures. When women live in small communities or even work in close environments, they often menstruate on the same schedule. Tribal women timed their cycles with the phases of the moon. Therefore, it is appropriate for us to celebrate the sacredness of our moon-blood as we explore the Moon mentor. Discuss your thoughts, feelings, and some experiences relating to your monthly cycle. Include your first menses and, if you have passed through the rite of menopause, your last. Do you see it as a cleansing or an energy flow? Describe how the bleeding-time makes you feel and, especially, what you do specifically for yourself during this sacred time.

Affirmation

Our beliefs create our reality. Write a personal affirmation that reflects your beliefs seen through the mirror of this major mentor. I have provided two for you, depending upon your gender.

Through the vehicle of my deepest emotions, I am carried unharmed through the dark night into the brilliant dawn.

Or

I embrace the entirety of my lunar splendor as maiden, mother, and crone.

Action

You have explored your thoughts and feelings by answering the questions above. This has been your inner work. Now, as part of your outer work, take some action! Perform an activity, action, or ritual that relates to the lessons of this card. It will help you to fully experience the message of the card as well as the aspect of yourself represented by the archetype. I have provided some examples. After completing the task, note your observations.

- Begin a dream journal. For an entire month, note the symbolism of your dreams as well as your intuitive impressions throughout the day.
- Go in the evening to a place that you normally visit during the day. Notice how the environment differs in the night. Take time to feel the subtleties and note your observations.
- Do something special exclusively with women. Embrace the camaraderie of these "sisters."
- Go to the ocean and gaze at the moon. Feel it pulling you with its lunar magnetism.

Art

Art touches the soul. Select a song, a poem, or a piece of art, literature, or film that relates to this card. Describe its relevance.

Mandala

In Chapter 4, you will create a personal tarot mandala. Select an image that exemplifies this card. Take a photograph or draw a picture. Choose an existing photo, a magazine picture, or an item that personally illustrates the card to you.

XIX. The Sun

Description

A happy, naked child holding a large, red banner rides upon a white horse. Behind the child is a walled garden brimming with beautiful, healthy sunflowers. The sun, in its splendor, shines brightly above them, like the Divine light that infuses the regenerated spirit. This is a card of profound optimism and success and represents rebirth and joy. Solar energy is masculine in nature (or yang) and corresponds to the dynamic element of fire. The banner in the illustration symbolizes victory and success. The horse represents the body and the forces of earth. And the child indicates innocence, freedom, and solar intelligence.

Self-Exploration

1. Look at the card and note how it makes you feel. Do you like this character?
2. The Sun card relates to the experience of shining forth and taking "center stage." It represents our moment in the proverbial spotlight, when we express our glory like the sun. When we experience hard times and our self-esteem is low, we forget our shining moments and focus, instead, on our mistakes and difficulties. At these critical moments, it would benefit us greatly to have a list of crowning achievements ready to reflect upon to remind us of our previous successes. Make a list of four such positive experiences to review whenever you have doubts about yourself. If you can list more than four, please do so (they can be little successes, too). Better yet, compile your own "brag book," or scrap book of achievements to help remind you of your accomplishments.

3. Solar (sun) energy, as opposed to lunar (moon) energy, is masculine in nature. We human beings contain aspects of ourselves that are both feminine and masculine. All people have within them an anima (yin) and an animus (yang) component. Is there a situation in your life that would best be handled with a surge of dynamic energy? Is there something you've been thinking too much about and now requires that you take action? In what way would this action allow you to regain a sense of personal power and bliss?

4. The Sun card symbolizes new opportunities, excellent health, and countless blessings. By taking time every day to enter into a state of gratitude, we reconnect with the source of our many blessings. We affirm our belief in universal abundance and open our hearts to spiritual and earthly bliss. In what ways do you give thanks? Do you regularly "count your blessings" or focus on gifts rather than adversity? Is there a time of day that you can designate for celebrating life by appreciation? Make a list of twenty things for which you are sincerely grateful.

5. On the spiritual path, we spend most of our time exploring our inner world. However, the body itself is considered the "temple of the soul" and also requires attention. The body, as a temple for our Divine Spark, requires that we make a commitment to its continuous health and wellness. Consider the way in which you express yourself physically. When is the last time you laughed and played—spontaneously and openly? Do you fully and openly express yourself sexually? The energy we project from our bodies is powerful and can have healing, liberating effects. Consider movement and dance and the way it makes you feel. Are you involved in the dance of life? Do you energize your body through athletics or exercise? How does it make you feel? Explore this issue and make a plan to allow your body to fully express itself.

Affirmation

Our beliefs create our reality. Write a personal affirmation that reflects your beliefs seen through the mirror of this major mentor. I have provided one for you.

I live in a radiant state of gratitude and bliss.

Action

You have explored your thoughts and feelings by answering the questions above. This has been your inner work. Now, as part of your outer work, take some action! Perform an activity, action, or ritual that relates to the lessons of this card. It will help you to fully experience the message of the card as well as the aspect of yourself represented by the archetype. I have provided some examples. After completing the task, note your observations.

- Run, play, dance, speak, make a presentation. Be center stage. Let yourself shine.
- Create a "brag book" of certificates, photos, expressions of gratitude, and other materials which illustrate former achievements. Look at your book at least once a month.
- Give thanks. Create a prayer of gratitude that you say at the beginning of the day, before meals, and at day's end.
- Add movement and exercise to your weekly routine.

Art

Art touches the soul. Select a song, a poem, or a piece of art, literature, or film that relates to this card. Describe its relevance.

Mandala

In Chapter 4, you will create a personal tarot mandala. Select an image that exemplifies this card. Take a photograph or draw a picture. Choose an existing photo, a magazine picture, or an item that personally illustrates the card to you.

XX. Judgement

Description

A magnificent, winged angel calls forth the dead from their tombs with the sound of his trumpet. The people, whose coffins float on the waters of the emotions and consciousness, raise their arms to receive forgiveness and eternal life. This card is associated with the Judeo-Christian concept of the Last Judgement, in which one's life is judged before God. The flag on the angel's trumpet is decorated with an equal-armed cross, indicating balance and equilibrium. The distant snowy mountains, symbolizing the need for further attainment,[14] illustrate that this is an ending and also a beginning in the soul's journey through consciousness.

Self-Exploration

1. Look at the card and note how it makes you feel. Do you like this character?

2. The Judgement card symbolizes closure and conclusion. As we move forward toward spiritual attainment, we strive to focus fully on the present and future. But, in order to do this effectively, we have to be sure we are not trailing unfinished business behind us. Unresolved issues can pull us into the past, filling us with negative feelings and concern. Do you need to make amends for past deeds or take care of unfinished business? What loose ends can you tie up in order to redirect your energies toward your present and your future? Is there something or someone you need to forgive?

3. After you have completed this life and have passed through death, how would you like to be remembered? What would you like your epitaph to say about your life's accomplishments?

4. The Judgement card describes eternal life with the Divine and a rebirth of consciousness. Many people have experienced profound illumination from what are called "near-death experiences." They describe spiritual epiphanies that occur when they are given the chance to return to their lives renewed. If we look at each day as a sort of rebirth, we can embrace this sense of renewal ourselves. Further, when we cease judging ourselves and forgive our past errors, we come away restored. Divine understanding transcends judgement while Divine healing transforms our very souls. What aspects of your past are you ready to forgive and let go of in order to receive Divine healing?

5. The concept of karma relates to the law of cause and effect—what we put out into the universe will come back to us many times over. What do you believe to be your life's purpose? What special contribution do you believe you were born to make? What is your bliss? Even if you are uncertain, explore this question and describe your thoughts and feelings about your soul's mission.

Affirmation

Our beliefs create our reality. Write a personal affirmation that reflects your beliefs seen through the mirror of this major mentor. I have provided one for you.

I forgive myself and others and eagerly receive the gift of Divine grace.

Action

You have explored your thoughts and feelings by answering the questions above. This has been your inner work. Now, as part of your outer work, take some action! Perform an activity, action, or ritual that relates to the lessons of this card. It will help you to fully experience the message of the card as well as the aspect of yourself represented by the archetype. I have provided some examples. After completing the task, note your observations.

- Forgive someone you have judged harshly. Then, forgive yourself for judging him/her. Acknowledge the healing power of Divine grace.
- Explore the phenomenon of near-death experiences. In what way are these experiences relevant to you?

- Visit a cemetery and read the epitaphs of people who are deceased. What strikes you most profoundly about the way they were remembered by the people who loved them?
- If you have found your life's purpose, take specific steps toward immersing yourself in it as soon as possible. If you are still searching, immerse yourself in something you absolutely love. Experience your bliss!

Art

Art touches the soul. Select a song, a poem, or a piece of art, literature, or film that relates to this card. Describe its relevance.

Mandala

In Chapter 4, you will create a personal tarot mandala. Select an image that exemplifies this card. Take a photograph or draw a picture. Choose an existing photo, a magazine picture, or an item that personally illustrates the card to you.

XXI. The World

Description

A beautiful woman, wearing only a banner to symbolize triumph, dances with rapture in the center of a woven oval-shaped wreath. She holds two wands in her outstretched hands (representing solar energy) and crosses her legs. Her gesture indicates the lower self surmounted by the higher self. Hovering in the clouds at the corners of the wreath are the symbols of earth, air, fire, and water. They represent the four elements and the four primary aspects of personality—sensation, thinking, intuition, and feeling. The dancer's transcendent expression illustrates spiritual awakening and transformation. Having journeyed through consciousness, she is now able to access her full potential. Her soul has attained full awareness of its Divine origins.

Self-Exploration

1. Look at the card and note how it makes you feel. Do you like this character?
2. The World card symbolizes the transcendent, ecstatic soul. It represents the cosmic consciousness within each of us which is completely aware of its Divine origin. What causes your spirit to dance? What brings you intense spiritual joy?
3. The World card speaks symbolically of the realization of a goal or the completion of a cycle. It suggests a new direction or a new universe—one that we have ourselves manifested. Indeed, as we change ourselves, we change the world around us. What kind of world would you manifest if you could create it yourself? Describe your thoughts in detail.

4. Everything in the universe is connected. There is unity all around us, even when we feel most isolated from it. In the beloved holiday film, "It's A Wonderful Life,"[15] the main character, George Bailey, meets an angel who gives him the opportunity to see what life would be like if he had never been born. He sees that the world is quite a different place without him and realizes that he has touched countless others in positive ways, without even knowing it. In what ways have you changed the world around you? Remember that even small things are like the ripples in a pond that radiate outward.

5. The World card represents mastery and attainment. After having viewed yourself through the "mirror" of the 22 tarot archetypes, what have you accomplished? What small goal has this exploration enabled you to attain? What greater spiritual goal do you now wish to achieve?

Affirmation

Our beliefs create our reality. Write a personal affirmation that reflects your beliefs seen through the mirror of this major mentor. I have provided one for you.

Everything I do matters greatly. I am one with the Universe.

Action

You have explored your thoughts and feelings by answering the questions above. This has been your inner work. Now, as part of your outer work, take some action! Perform an activity, action, or ritual that relates to the lessons of this card. It will help you to fully experience the message of the card as well as the aspect of yourself represented by the archetype. I have provided some examples. After completing the task, note your observations.

• This is a new beginning. Do something to affirm your new life, new beliefs, and new spiritual focus.

• Finish something that needs finishing. Feel the satisfaction associated with completion.

• Do something that brings you intense spiritual joy and reflect on how vital and alive it makes you feel.

• Take specific steps toward making the world a better place by getting involved in an effort that will help to make it happen. Commit to making a significant personal contribution to the effort. Co-creation is our birthright. So create your world, starting now.

Art

Art touches the soul. Select a song, a poem, or a piece of art, literature, or film that relates to this card. Describe its relevance.

Mandala

In Chapter 4, you will create a personal tarot mandala. Select an image that exemplifies this card. Take a photograph or draw a picture. Choose an existing photo, a magazine picture, or an item that personally illustrates the card to you.

Chapter 3

Pathworking: Tools for Transformation

Practical Applications

By gazing deeply into the 22 mirrors of the tarot's major mentors, you have gleaned valuable information about the aspects of yourself that they represent. You have done some considerable soul-searching and self-exploration. You have taken action to affirm the spiritual steps you've taken. Now, it's time to learn some practical, effective ways to apply your new-found knowledge and experience. You will soon learn techniques to effectively deepen your level of spiritual insight and create positive change in your life.

Growth and Change

As individuals and as a society, we are constantly in a state of flux and process. We are forever reinventing ourselves, creating new layers of belief and personality, while systematically stripping away the old and outmoded. We work toward becoming more authentic by integrating the genuine into our selves. We earnestly endeavor to expel falsity and illusion. And as we come closer to realizing personal authenticity, we come closer to touching the Divine Spark within us. This is the kind of growth that really makes a difference.

Positive Influences

Positive influences can greatly inspire our process. As we recreate ourselves and refocus our energies toward spiritual attainment, we can use the mentors of the tarot like archetypal role models. These imaginary, symbolic teachers can be used to represent those critical aspects of ourselves that need to be brought into the light. The images of the tarot can assist you in many ways by providing the following:

- Insight and inspiration
- A focal point for concentration and contemplation (stepping stones to meditation)
- Focus and strength while facing a challenge
- "Seed" for thoughts and dreams
- Guidance and direction (you could ask yourself, for example, "What would the Empress do?")
- Tools for inner understanding.

Techniques for Using the Mentors

The following are some specific techniques for using the major mentors of the tarot to provide guidance and insight on your path. This is only a brief sampling to get you started. The tarot images are extremely effective tools that can assist you in your quest for inner transformation. So, I encourage you to discover your own unique methods of using the images for your own pathworking purposes.

A. Painting a Picture of your Spiritual Path

You have identified your spiritual goals. You have some ideas about where you are now and where you want to be. Use this effective technique to gain clarity about the nature of your spiritual path and your current course of action.

Place your cards in front of you. Look at all 22 images and consciously choose the card that most aptly describes your current spiritual state or inner environment. Then, choose a card to represent where you want to be—your goal. Remember that process is dynamic. Your goals today may not be your goals in the distant future. This is why you can use the following simple technique over and over again, at different points of your life, to clarify and redirect your course. After choosing the card that best symbolizes the spiritual state you are seeking, choose the card that symbolizes the transition. The transition card is the one that can help you to turn your "current" card into your "goal" card. Here's an example of the thought process:

Where I am now: The Tower

("Everything in my life is falling apart. It's a real mess.")

Where I want to be: The Empress

("I want to fully experience myself as a creative, abundant, loving, nurturing woman. Love is my best conveyance to the Divine.")

Transition card to get there: The Hermit

("Turning within and embracing my inner silence will help illuminate that light within me. Only then will I be reborn as The Empress. Like the caterpillar that needs the solitary, nurturing environment of the cocoon to help it transform into the butterfly, I need to find my place of inner solitude and peace. This is the action I need to take.")

If it is difficult for you to choose your transition card, choose several cards and mentally/emotionally try them on for size. Does one feel better than the others or make more sense when you think it through? What does your intuition say? Eventually, choose the one card that best describes the manner in which you can achieve the state you desire.

At the conclusion of this process, the three cards you have chosen will create a symbolic road map for your spiritual journey. So, instead of asking the cards what will happen in the future, as in the process of divination, you are using your focus and intention to *create* your future. You are using your will and sense of purpose to prioritize your life and clarify your spiritual steps. Place the cards side by side and take some quality time to study them:

CURRENT	TRANSITION	GOAL

B. Creating Major Changes in Your Life

Making major changes requires that you address various, complex aspects of your beliefs and behavior. You need to devise a plan that approaches the process from many different angles. One way you can ease your process is to allow the mentors to provide guidance and inspiration.

Say, for example, your wellness and fitness level is not where you want it to be and you need to make some serious changes in your lifestyle. You have decided to drastically change your weekly routine to include a healthy diet, regular exercise, and stress management. This is just an example. In your case, it could be anything. Maybe you're going back to college or going through the break-up of a relationship or expanding your level of religious involvement/devotion. Perhaps you're training intensely for a music recital or deciding to become an emotionally stronger individual, or even committing to fighting an addiction. Your life change could be anything at all. The sky's the limit.

Choose seven cards to help provide insight and guidance for each of the seven days of the week. You may choose seven cards to correspond to seven different aspects of the change you wish to make. For example, the Emperor is a good choice if you wish to become a better leader, or the Empress if you wish to become more loving and nurturing. You may also choose cards that relate to some daily action. For example, the Sun card could be chosen for the day you designate for exercise; Temperance might be chosen for the day you dedicate to meditative activities; the Heirophant might be a good choice for Sunday or Saturday, if you regularly attend religious services.

Most important is that you choose seven cards for seven days of the week. Simply choose the cards that you feel are the most meaningful mentors for the task ahead. You know yourself and the personal challenges ahead of you. You also know where you may feel a weakness that needs strengthening. Choose the mentors that represent the aspects of yourself that need to be strong in order to achieve your goal. For example, if stress is a problem for you, you might find the Temperance card to be helpful. If depression and hopelessness are unwelcome companions, choose the image of the Star for hope and inspiration. If you lack discipline or structure, try the Heirophant or the Emperor. And if you need strength or courage, choose the Strength or Chariot card.

After you have chosen your cards, write an affirmation that relates to the specific message of the card. For example, The Star provides hope in a difficult situation. So, if you are seeking to rectify a difficult situation in your life, the affirmation for this card might be "There is always hope," "I am bathed in the grace of God," or even "I can do this. I am loved." The affirmation is useful in providing a specific, conscious message, while the tarot image provides a symbolic message to the subconscious mind.

Start a journal. Use a blank book from your local bookstore or a spiral-bound notebook filled with lined paper. If you are on your computer often throughout the day, you could create a file for this purpose. Use whatever suits you, but choose a journal that will be dedicated exclusively to your current process. This is an important change in your life and you give a powerful message to yourself when you create a special place for recording your progress. You can also look back on your writings later, to learn more about yourself and your growth. Be diligent about writing something every day to maintain momentum.

In the beginning of the book, write your name and the date. Title the journal. In our example, the title could be something like "Health and Wellness Journal." Write a page or more about your current state and why you are choosing to make such a profound change in your life. Be honest about why you are unhappy with your current situation. It will be helpful to review this information to strengthen your resolve when you're feeling less strong or committed. It is very common for our resolve to waver when times are difficult. Write down your plan, if you have one, and be positive about your commitment. If you have created a new routine for yourself, describe it, including the new activities you have planned for yourself (e.g., Saturday morning—meditate for 30 minutes before breakfast. Wednesday 6:00 P.M.—attend yoga class). On a separate page, one that you will keep marked for easy reference, write down the names of the seven days of the week and the seven tarot mentors you have chosen for each of the days. Next to the mentor titles, write the corresponding affirmation and specify what beneficial characteristics the card represents for you.

At the beginning of each day, contemplate the image you have chosen. Put it on the bathroom mirror where you can look at it while you are preparing yourself for the day. Place the card in a book, if you are reading or studying, where you will see it often. Place it on your refrigerator or dresser. Keep it in your pocket, purse, wallet, desk drawer, car, or any place where you will see it often. Or, simply place it in your journal for safe keeping. In your journal, begin a new page with the date, the day of the week, and the tarot card for the day. Write the affirmation, to remind you of the message of the card. Read the affirmation often throughout the day. Ideally, you can use the journal throughout the day. If this is not practical for you, simply fill it in before going to bed. Describe in writing any difficulties you experienced that day, as well as any successes. It is important to validate the little victories you experience when you are making life changes. Jot down the ways in which the image of the tarot card provided inspiration, insight, or a new perspective you have gained during the day. Then, look at the card one more time before going to bed, planting a positive seed for your dreams.

As you continue this process every day, you will find that you are greatly assisted by the messages of the cards. With this kind of regular focus, you will be surprised to see blooming within yourself, the very aspects or positive characteristics the mentors symbolize.

This is what your journal pages might look like if you were going to make the health and wellness changes described in our example.

Health and Wellness Journal
Tarot/Affirmation Page

Sundays   *The Star*: Hope.
"I can do this. I am loved."

Mondays   *The Heirophant*: Structure, discipline.

"I have a plan."

Tuesdays *The Hanged Man:* New perspective, self-sacrifice.
"I see things in a new way. I am ready to rise to the next level."

Wednesdays *The Magician:* Self-Control, Manifestation.
"As within, so without. And so it is."

Thursdays *The Tower:* Blast away old beliefs and patterns.
"The past does not equal the future. I wipe the slate clean to begin anew."

Fridays *Strength:* Feminine strength, love.
"I am worthy of wellness and fitness. Strength is beautiful."

Saturdays *Temperance:* Inner serenity
"Life flows through me with ease. I am bathed in peace."

Daily Page

Monday: *The Heirophant*
Focus: Structure, discipline.
Affirmation: "I have a plan."

Daily intake:
Breakfast: Hot 5 grain cereal w/nonfat soy milk and maple syrup, orange juice
Snack: Fuji apple
Lunch: Vegetable-cous-cous wrap, split pea soup
Snack: Air-popped popcorn topped with nori sea vegetable flakes
Dinner: Mushroom risotto, steamed asparagus, beets, vege baked beans
Snack: 2 fat free fig bars and herbal tea

Total fat: *8 grams*
Water: 3 bottles/48 ounces
Exercise: Step aerobics class - 1 hour
Stress Mgt: Hot bath before bed with candles and Native American flute music

Comments: Difficult today, but I'm proud of myself for rising to the occasion, maintaining my commitment, and sticking to my fitness regime. Friends at work invited me out for the weekly pizza and beer night and I almost gave in. I was tired after a really stressful day. But, I promised myself a healthy dinner and a hot bath after my aerobics class instead. I also wanted to forgo the opportunity to contribute to the rumor mill. Listening to and spreading gossip is a behavior that I really don't want to encourage—in myself or others. I don't want to make false judgments about people, or have them made about me. Anyway, I'm making my own choices about how I want to use my precious time and energy and I feel good about taking a stand for a change.

The Heirophant provided inspiration to me today by reminding me of the importance of structure and discipline if I want to see results. His image also helped me to feel dignified and strong enough to pass on the evening of gossip and overindulgence. The Heirophant encourages me to focus on the teachers/mentors of my life. Next week, I think I'm going to stay after class and talk with my aerobics instructor. I think she's very knowledgeable about physiology and probably has some great suggestions to enhance my wellness plan. She's so fit and full of energy, as well as being very feminine. She's a real inspiration. There's another thing about the Heirophant. When I look at the illustration on the card, I think about some of the traditional teachings I grew up with as a young Catholic girl. I find myself thinking of the powerful simplicity of some of the moral guidelines and remembering some of the prayers we repeated over and over again. Although I have adopted a different, less rigid theology as an adult, it's wonderfully affirming to validate the childhood lessons that still resonate with truth for me.

C. Focusing Your Energy

Suppose you want to integrate a certain mentor characteristic into your personality or to simply focus on something that is important to you. As in the previous example, choose the card or cards that represent the influences you are seeking. Here are some examples of mentors that would be useful for specific purposes. Each of the 22 mentors can provide inspiration in a multitude of ways. I have listed only a few as examples.

Cultivate your leadership potential: *The Emperor*
Learn to nurture others and express yourself more lovingly: *The Empress*
Infuse your life with gratitude and praise to the Divine: *The Star*
Be more disciplined and structured in your studies: *The Heirophant*
Integrate contemplation/meditation into your life: *The Hermit*
Become less judgmental and critical of others/yourself: *Judgment*
Let go of a situation that is no longer constructive: *Death*
Deal with a difficult or challenging situation/person: *Strength*

When you have chosen the card or cards to represent your new area of focus, place the card in a position of prominence in your home, office, or on your person. It is always helpful to view the image periodically throughout the day, but if it is not possible (or appropriate), simply look at the card in the morning and at night. Even a word printed in a prime location can remind you to focus your mind toward your goal. When I was working in a difficult office environment some years ago, I changed the initial computer prompt at my work station to remind me of the Strength card. I found it to be extremely helpful in keeping me focused on my ability to handle the situation.

D. Daily Messages

At the beginning of each day, use your intuition to select a card at random from your stack of 22 major arcana tarot cards. Fan them out upside down and select one. Shuffle them, cut them, and choose one. Use whatever method appeals to you. Keep in mind that, in studying the card you have chosen, you are planting a subconscious seed that will invariably sprout during the day. You could ask yourself the question, "How can the lessons of this card assist me on my path today?" And, during the day, be mindful of the response(s) you receive. I would be very surprised if you didn't find the lessons of your chosen card to be particularly relevant to you at some time during the day.

This exercise can serve as a refresher course for you as well. You may find that you have favorite cards within the tarot deck and tend to gravitate toward them. As a result, you may find that you don't spend a great deal of time, energy, or focus on certain other cards. Feel free to consciously choose those other cards as daily lesson cards. Take the opportunity to deepen your understanding of their message for you. Every image has a lesson or experience for you, so be sure to spend some time focusing on every one of the 22 cards. And remember, it's your process. Use whatever method feels right for you.

Chapter 4

Creating Your Personal Tarot Mandala

Creative Fun

It's time to pull together all the images you've collected for your mandala and have some creative fun. You're going to create your own, personal tarot mandala. You have chosen images from magazines or photographs or perhaps even drawn pictures of your own. Each image is like your own personal tarot card—a specific representation of the 22 major mentors. By placing all of the personal images together, you will create a piece of art that reflects crucial aspects of your inner and outer self. It will also provide you with a magical, aesthetic symbol of your total self and spiritual journey.

What is a Mandala?

The word mandala is a Sanskrit word meaning center and circle.[16] Mandalas are used in many cultures and can be viewed in such diverse forms as Tibetan Buddhist religious designs, Navajo sand paintings, Neolithic spiral patterns, Celtic religious illustrations, and Hindu tatwa designs. The periphery of these intricate designs brings the viewing eye on a sort of journey to the center of the design. That center represents the point of power or place of oneness within the Universe. The periphery is the path leading you to that point of power. Together, they symbolize the totality of our beings. Carl Jung called mandalas our "eternal mind's eternal recreation," or the path to our center.[17]

Like the rings of a tree trunk or the ripples in a pond after dropping a stone, our lives create mandalas. Our centers reflect our places of origin and our immortal souls, while the outer ripples reflect our outward journeys through existence.

A. Creating Your Own Mandala

Place the pictures you have chosen in front of you and decide how you want to label them. You may wish to attach a label to them or write on the pictures themselves. You might like to glue the pictures to some labeled card stock as a background so it looks like an actual card. In order for you to associate the image with the archetype from the tarot cards, write the name of the card ("The Star," for example) and/or the number of the card somewhere on the picture. It is important to give each picture a title, though, linking it to the traditional tarot, thereby making the message personally relevant for you.

After you have given titles to your pictures, you will need to choose a format for your mandala. You may wish to use a collage format or something more structured. It is entirely up to you. Choose a design that is meaningful for you. This does not have to be a rigid or structured type of design. A random collage format is artistic, intuitive, and a great deal of fun to create. In a collage, the pictures tumble around each other in a free and expressive manner. Other items can be glued on to enhance a collage such as stones, feathers, or dried flowers. Rather than a collage, you may, instead, choose to use an actual design that is significant for you. You could use a background to fill in or create a design with the pictures themselves. Your only limitation is your creative genius. Here are some examples of formats to get your creative juices flowing.

1. *Collage*: Use a random method of gluing down the pictures in a way that is pleasing and artistic to you, without trying to describe a particular image or design. Use your intuition and be childlike in your play. You could glue the pictures to a blank page if you would find that to be less distracting, or you could use a colored background, solid or designed. I have personally used a background of magazine pictures of natural beauty to make collages. This way, if there is a space between the pictures, I have trees, oceans, flowers, or

mountains as a glorious backdrop.

2. *Enhance an Existing Image*: Choose a background that is particularly significant for you and place the 22 images in relevant positions on the existing background. For example, the Hebrew Kaballah provides a profound glyph called the Tree of Life. Within this "tree" are spheres or sephira, each representing a realm of spiritual experience. Each tarot card can be attributed to a sphere on the Tree. If the study of the Kaballah is meaningful for you, you could draw the glyph and place the pictures in their appropriate places. Other examples might be to use a Native American shield, placing the tarot images within the quadrants of the four directions or to use a personal astrological chart, placing the images within the houses that are relevant for you. You could even use the human body as a backdrop and place the images on the areas that are appropriate for you. Which image would you place in your heart, above your head, or in your hands? The possibilities abound!

3. *Create a Design*: Use the pictures to create a special design by gluing them down artistically. For example, you could start with the Fool in the center, then radiate out with the other pictures to create a flower, a sun, a fan, or a bird. You could choose pictures to form a trunk and others to signify branches and create the design of a tree. You could spell out a letter or initials. You could create a geometric design that delights the eye and stirs the soul. How about putting the images around a wheel, so you could turn it to choose a card for the day? The only limit is your imagination.

4. *Progressive Lineup*: The major mentors of the tarot, set side-by-side, tell a dramatic spiritual story of inner metamorphosis. As we move from the experience of one card to that of the next card, we move our consciousness to the next level of awakening and understanding. You may find it meaningful to place your pictures in the exact order that they occur in the tarot. For example, the Fool, Number 0, would be first, followed by the Magician, Number 1. Follow with Numbers 2 through 20. The last card, then, would be the World, Number 21. In this way, you could see the mentors in their given order, as a sort of continuum.

5. *Transformational Art*: My friend's little boy has a terrific toy. He can

use it to describe his mood for the day using various faces. The faces can be moved into different pockets within a circle or be chosen for the central "this is how I feel today" position. As an adult, you could use your archetypal pictures to reflect the way you're expressing yourself at any given moment. You could even use it to reflect your current challenge or area of attention. If you were to use a removable mounting substance, you could create a mandala that changes as you change. For example, one central picture could symbolize your primary focus. You could then place the pictures representing synergistic influences in an inner ring around the central image. The less-related images could remain in the outer circle until they are moved into a position of prominence at some other time. Your mandala would be a changing, dynamic art piece, one that reflects your own inner transformation at any given moment.

B. Using Your Mandala

Now that you have created a piece of artwork that is intensely personal and deeply significant, let's discuss some of the ways you can use it in your own daily pathworking. Creating the personal tarot mandala was as powerful action. Contemplating the mandala's significance is even more profound. The following is a description of the technique of physically and mentally preparing yourself for contemplation. This process can be used whenever you wish to focus on an individual tarot card as well.

1. *Creating a Suitable Environment*: Several factors are important to consider when you are preparing to contemplate your newly created mandala. First, create an environment that is conducive to relaxation and easy concentration (easy concentration as opposed to the concentration you associate with hard work, as in your office). Go to the room that you choose when you want to "get away from it all," if such a room exists in your home. If no such room exists, find a way to create a sacred space for yourself so you may use it for this purpose. Ask the members of your household not to disturb you for the time you have designated. Close the door, unplug the phone, remove clutter and distracting items from your line of vision. Choose a comfortable place to sit, where your spine can be straight and your

body can be comfortable. Some people sit comfortably on the floor, while others prefer to sit in a chair. I only caution you against lying down, because your body might think you are seeking to induce sleep, rather than illumination. Place your mandala in front of you, where you can see it clearly and effortlessly. Reduced light can do a great deal to create a relaxed setting, but don't use candles and low lighting to such an extent that you make it difficult to see the detail of your mandala. You shouldn't be straining to see in front of you.

2. *Body*: The first order of business in any contemplative or meditative effort is to relax your body and focus your attention on your breathing. While you are maintaining excellent posture, mentally move your attention from the tips of your toes all the way up to the top of your head, instructing your body to relax at each interval. For example, you might affirm, "My toes and feet are relaxed. My ankles are relaxed. My legs are heavy and completely relaxed," etc. Your body will obey your commands and will adopt a state of repose. When you have achieved the desired state of relaxation, your mind will be better able to focus on the object before you without distraction. Use whatever imaginative method you find to be effective in inducing this level of relaxation, such as visualization.

3. *Grounding*: After your body is relaxed, visualize a cord running down the base of your spine, down through the earth, where it fastens itself securely to a peg at the center of the earth. Use whatever imagery you wish to use, as long as it effectively symbolizes a grounding process. Feel firmly attached to the earth, firmly in control of your process.

4. *Affirmation/Prayer*: Place your hands on your lap, with palms open, and take a deep cleansing breath. Affirm and/or pray—mentally or verbally. The purpose of this step is to prepare yourself for the process and to affirm your Divine Source. In order to clear myself for the work ahead, I first use the following cleansing affirmation: "I believe in the evolution of the soul and now release all energy that is not my own and return it to its source with love and healing." I then use this simple prayer to affirm my Divine source in English and/or Hebrew, "In your hands is the kingdom, the power, and the glory, now and forever." You could use an affirmation such as, "I resolve to ignite the

Divine spark within me by moving ever closer to God(dess)."
Marion Weinstein gives a wonderful "formula" for creating words of
power (affirmations) in her book, *Positive Magic*.[18] I have personally
adapted her words of power as follows and encourage you to adapt
them for your own needs. "There is One Power, which is
God/Goddess, and which is perfect fulfillment. My heart resonates
with this power. Therefore, spiritual fulfillment is mine, here and
now. For the good of all, according to the free will of all. And so it
is." Choose whatever words of power speak sincerely from your heart.
Pray in the manner that affirms your Divine source.

5. *Breathing*: Devote as much time as you can spare to focusing entirely
   on your breathing. Close your eyes and become acutely aware of the
   breath coming in and the breath coming out. Exhale any residual
   tension you might be feeling, while you inhale relaxation and focus.
   Exhale distraction while you inhale attention and *intention*. I have
   found that visualizing the breath moving in an egg-shaped manner is
   very helpful in creating a meditative state. Imagine your breath
   flowing down the front of the body, under the seat, and up the back
   of the spine to the top of the head and down again. Inhale up the
   spine and exhale down the front of your body. You will be focusing
   your breath as you move your energy (chi or life force) from the base
   of the spine up to the nape of the neck. When you have reached your
   head, begin exhaling so gently that you barely realize that you are
   releasing your breath. The shift from exhalation to inhalation at the
   seat should be handled just as gently. The egg-shaped breathing will
   help you feel like you are bathed in a cocoon of cleansing, healing
   light and breath. You may prefer the simple visualization of the
   breath and energy moving up the spine as you inhale, and down the
   spine as your exhale.[19]

6. *Preparing the Mind*: Your body is relaxed. You are grounded and have
   affirmed your point of power and purpose. You have focused
   sufficiently on your breathing and have achieved a state that is
   receptive and clear. Now, you are ready to focus your mind on your
   tarot mandala (or individual tarot image). As you begin to look at
   the mandala, you may find that your mind begins to misbehave.
   Meditators call this phenomenon "monkey mind" The mind is

accustomed to throwing random thoughts at you whenever it wishes. It doesn't like being placed on hold while you concentrate. All of a sudden, you find yourself reviewing something a person said to you earlier in the day and you find your mind racing haphazardly. When this happens, you've got a sure case of monkey mind. Your defense against this challenge is a simple one. *Acknowledge the thought and send it on its way.* Rather than pretending the thought isn't there, tell the mind, "yes, I'll consider that later." Then, get back to the business of concentrating on your mandala.

7. *Concentration*: Concentration usually follows contemplation. But, in our case, we are going to concentrate on our mandala as seed or inspiration for our contemplation. Gaze at your mandala. Resist the temptation to look at anything else in the room. Take some time to concentrate on the center of your mandala. While you are gazing at the center, your peripheral vision will catch glimpses of the outer images. After sufficiently focusing on the center point, allow your eyes to explore the mandala. Look at the images from a variety of angles. Begin from the outside and work in toward the center. Gaze at the top portion, the center, and then the bottom. Take note if you find yourself returning to certain images over and over again. Are certain images brighter or more vibrant to you? After you have gazed at your mandala from every angle, close your eyes.

8. *Contemplation*: With your eyes closed, allow thoughts to enter your mind pertaining to the tarot mandala. If, while contemplating the mandala, your mind begins to digress, bring it back to the subject at hand. This technique requires mental discipline. Contemplate what you have taken in through your eyes and take note of any patterns or especially significant images. What new insights or associations are coming to you? Is a situation clearer as seen through the mirror of the tarot images?

9. *Meditation*: If you wish, you may move to a state of meditation by endeavoring to remove all thoughts from your mind. Consider this a receptive or listening state. Again, usher out your random thoughts, assuring them that they will have a valid audience later. Return your attention to your breathing and settle into the warmth of the darkness behind your eyelids. You may wish to focus on the point

between your eyes or to simply relax into your breathing. Say your prayer or affirmation once again, if you are having trouble focusing. Take several deep breaths, and move into a deeper state of receptivity. Then listen. True meditation is a state of "no mind," where you are initiating no thoughts whatsoever. Let go and be still, inside and out. Meditation is a wonderful opportunity to receive guidance, insight, and healing from whatever you believe your Divine source to be. It's also a time for embracing tranquility and peace.

10. *Gradual Return*: After meditating, you will need to return your consciousness to its former state. Do not do this abruptly, unless it is absolutely necessary. It is best to take as much time as you can to focus on bringing your awareness back to your body and your conscious mind. Again, pay attention to your breath as you inhale and exhale rhythmically. Wiggle your toes and fingers and move your attention to your rested, but now alert, body and mind. If you are feeling foggy or sleepy, visualize your breath moving down the spine to form a glowing ball of light at the base of the spine. Take your hands and place them on your solar plexus. This is your power center. Imagine infusing your center with a bright, clear yellow light. Open your eyes and regain your awareness of the room. Are you aware of heat or cold or even a scent in the room? Bring your mundane senses back into focus, move your body, and greet your day renewed.

11. *Heightened Awareness*: After having experienced your mandala on a whole new level, your subconscious mind may have some new information to share with you. Pay close attention to your insights and dreams after you have performed your contemplation or meditation exercise. The exercise is a deepening experience and very much like opening a door that has previously been bolted shut. There are marvelous insights and great understanding to be gained when you walk through that open door.

Taking Inventory and Continuing the Journey

Over the past days or weeks or months, while you experienced the process outlined in the previous chapters, you have made immeasurable progress. By turning and searching within as well as by boldly expressing yourself in the world, you made a profound statement about the importance of your personal spiritual experience. You prioritized your journey toward the Divine. You reflected. You searched your soul for answers to important questions and honestly defined your beliefs. You resolved. You made conscious decisions about what you are capable of and affirmed your values. You created. You found inspiration through art and, through the ancient art form of the mandala, visually expressed your inner process. You contemplated. You focused your heart and mind toward your spiritual goals, while clarifying your own, personal truth. You powerfully affirmed the relevance of the Divine in your life.

Through your efforts, you have taken faithful steps toward your spiritual Source. You have made a significant beginning. Now, the real fun begins. It's time for you to continue your journey in earnest. If your self-exploration has revealed a clear path for you to follow, then run, don't walk, down that path! If your self-exploration has made you eager for more information or more inspiration, I urge you to go out and get it! Information and inspiration are both well within your reach. Learn more and continue to grow ever closer to embracing your Divine birthright. Read, take classes, and become involved in activities that encourage you to embrace your spiritual nature. Remember that the Divine is inclusive, not exclusive. If you are unsure during your journey, turn to your own heart. Nobody can do that as well as you can. Listening to your heart will keep you on track better than a guru or a group who offers easy answers, but squelches your inner fire. And if, after seeking, you're still not sure which path to follow, simply maintain momentum and keep the fires of inspiration burning brightly. Keep seeking and loving and listening. You will find what you're looking for.

My *purpose* in writing this book is to empower you to seek and embrace your own path to the Divine. I truly believe that the Divine reveals him/herself to each of us in unique and wondrous ways, and we must continue to seek until we recognize that unmistakable Truth. It has been my privilege to share my heart and my thoughts with you. I bow to your Atman, your Divine self.

References

1. *Rider-Waite Tarot Deck*, designed by Pamela Colman Smith under the direction of Arthur Edward Waite, U.S. Games Systems, Inc., New York, NY, 1971.

2. *Motherpeace Tarot Deck*, Karen Vogel and Vicki Noble, U.S. Games Systems, Inc., Stamford, CT, 1981.

3. *The Dictionary of the Tarot*, Bill Butler, Schocken Books, New York, NY, 1975, p. 3.

4. *Positive Magic: Occult Self-Help*, Marion Weinstein, Phoenix Publishing Co, Custer, WA, Revised Edition, 1978, 1981, p. 178.

5. *The Royal Road: A Manual of Kabalistic Meditations on the Tarot*, Stephan A. Hoeller, The Theosophical Publishing House, Wheaton, IL, 1975, p. 88.

6. *The Dictionary of the Tarot*, Bill Butler, Schocken Books, New York, NY, 1975, p. 117.

7.-14. *The Royal Road: A Manual of Kabalistic Meditations on the Tarot*, Stephan A. Hoeller, The Theosophical Publishing House, Wheaton, IL, 1975, pp. 96, 90, 94, 82, 80, 70, 62, 64.

15. "It's a Wonderful Life", directed and produced by Frank Capra for Liberty Films and RKO Studios, starring James Stewart and Donna Reed, 1946.

16. *Everyone's Mandala Coloring Book*, Monique Mandali, Mandali Publishing, Billings, MT, Revised Edition, 1978, 1991, p.1.

17. Ibid.

18. *Positive Magic: Occult Self-Help*, Marion Weinstein, Phoenix Publishing Co, Custer, WA, Revised Edition, 1981, page 216.

19. Breathing and meditation techniques credited to the pranayama instruction of Edmond Boles, Amron Metaphysical Center, San Francisco, California.

Acknowledgements

Thank you, Divine Source, for creating the inner longing that compels me to seek you.

To my husband, Terry, thank you for being a steadfast champion in helping me pursue my bliss. You have the soul of an artist and the depth of a mystic. To Sarah and Shannon, our beautiful, radiant daughters, thank you for your unconditional love. May you find peace and power in claiming your spiritual birthright and never lose sight of the Divine spark within you.

I owe a great debt of gratitude to the many teachers who have guided me in my spiritual journey, especially Rev. Edmond Boles, Rev. Norma Tringali, Rev. Sandy Winter, Rev. Mark Gallagher, and Rev. Nel Stiling. I also appreciate the countless authors who have been inspirational teachers to me throughout the years, particularly Stephan A. Hoeller, author of *The Royal Road: A Manual of Kabalistic Meditations on the Tarot*, whose insights and eloquence assisted me immeasurably in writing this book.

Many thanks to the kind souls who agreed to read, review, and listen to the book in varying forms and stages. Many thanks to Lioness Books in Sacramento, CA and the students of my women's spirituality classes who contributed much to this book. Working with Jackie and Gretchen Hofer at SunShine Press Publications has been a privilege and a pleasure. I am truly grateful for their leap of faith.

I love my family fiercely and must thank them individually for their love and support. Special thanks to my Mom, the remarkable, capable woman who was my very first teacher and who has loved me all the days of my life; to my Dad for being such a loving Grandad to our little ones; to B.P. and to Di for their love and strength. Thanks to my siblings for inspiring me: Lynn, with her creativity and wisdom; Bob, with his dedication to music and consciousness; Penny, with her incredible mind and wit and for urging me to grow where I was planted; and Tammy, with her compassionate heart and brilliant humor. To Tanis, my extraordinary sister-in-law, thank you for sharing your heart and for bringing me the joy of your love and friendship.

Many thanks to my parents in-law, Jean and Jim, for their loving kindness, generosity, and steadfast devotion to our family. Thank you, Cousin Lorna for your kind generosity. You helped to turn this dream into a reality. Last, I wish to thank my Aunt Grace who never failed to find the time to remind me of my gifts or potential. Thank you for your loving encouragement over these many years.

Finally, I couldn't have written this book without the love and support of my dear friends. I can't mention them all, but wish to specifically thank Diane Holliday for encouraging me to write this book; Debbie Ruh, for loving me through thick and thin for 28 years; Barbara Boss for her unique cover art and tender, loving care; Laurie Cory for her love and friendship; Afsaneh Martin for her warmth, laughter, and love; Cindy Click for her sensitivity and kindness and for sharing my initial book drafts in China; Nga Pham for exemplifying courage, generosity, and loving kindness; Kit Lucey for her warmth and words of empowerment; Colleen Sheehan for the "important questions" we posed together so many years ago; and Tracey Gray for joyfully sharing my first class on the tarot as archetypes at the *Well Women's Centre* in Western Australia.

About the Author

Diane Toland has been exploring comparative theology and belief systems for over 25 years. She has travelled extensively, piecing together the mysteries of this miracle we call life. She has studied t'ai chi chuan, t'ai chi chih, karate, yoga, and qi gong. She has gratefully received instruction in many spiritual traditions: tarot, hermetic magic, kaballah, meditation, energy healing, pranayama and motherhood.

Diane has a passion for teaching and has provided instruction in a variety of topics including English, Massage for Couples, Awakening the Goddess Within, Archetypes for the Spiritual Journey, Manifestation, and Balancing the Shadow. She has made her home and classroom in three countries: China, Australia, and the United States.

Diane is a certified massage therapist, infant massage instructor, and holistic health educator. She enjoys music, literature, art, needlepoint and nature.